The Reality Between

The Reality Between

❖

A Buddhist Approach to
Addiction, Grief, and Psychotherapy

Kenneth A. Lucas

iUniverse, Inc.
New York Lincoln Shanghai

The Reality Between
A Buddhist Approach to Addiction, Grief, and Psychotherapy

All Rights Reserved © 2004 by Kenneth A. Lucas

No part of this book may be reproduced or transmitted in any form or by any means, graphic, electronic, or mechanical, including photocopying, recording, taping, or by any information storage retrieval system, without the written permission of the publisher.

iUniverse, Inc.

For information address:
iUniverse, Inc.
2021 Pine Lake Road, Suite 100
Lincoln, NE 68512
www.iuniverse.com

ISBN: 0-595-32149-6

Printed in the United States of America

In memory of my grandmother, Maude Ella Burch Lucas (1889–1979), who gave me unconditional love.

Reality Between*: One of the six betweens, named in that way due to the fact that the individual experiencing it is as close as he can get to the realization of the liberating reality of freedom…*
 —Robert A. F. Thurman, *The Tibetan Book of the Dead*

We must seriously enter into the experience of the sands slipping away in the hourglass of our lives. This discomforting feeling of the unstoppable dimming of the light, the numbering of breaths, must be embraced until it hurts.
 —Eugene Bianchi, *Aging As a Spiritual Journey*

CONTENTS

Preface xiii
Introduction xv

CHAPTER 1 Our Flight from The Truth of Impermanence 1
    Unsettling *Between* States and Ever-Present Change 1
    Why We Don't Acknowledge Impermanence 2
    Persistent Evidence of Impermanence 8
    The Price We Pay for Denial 10
    Embracing The Truth of Impermanence 11
    Recognizing the Centrality of *Between* States 13
    Examples of Acute *Bardo* States 14
    Examples of Chronic *Bardo* States 14
    Examples of Other *Between* States 15

CHAPTER 2 The Rise of Grief Models 16
    Buddhism's View of Grief 16
    Early Griefwork Models: Freud, Bowlby, and Parkes 18
    Task Models of Grief: Lindemann, Worden, and Rando 19
    The Process Model of Grief: Kübler-Ross 20
    Application of Grief Stages to Non-Death Grieving 22

CHAPTER 3 Using Grief Stages in Individual Psychotherapy 24
    Recognizing Patients' *Between* States 24
    Anger As a Grief Stage 27
    Depression As a Grief Stage 29
    Who Is Allowed to Grieve and Who Isn't 30
    Interactions with Those in Other Grief Stages 31
    Understanding "Control Freaks" in Terms of *Bardo* States 32

Self-Esteem and *Bardo* States 33
Viewing Neurosis and Psychosis in Terms of *Bardo* States 34
Guiding Patients from Content to Process 36
Frankl's "Sunday Neurosis" As a *Bardo* State 37
About the Word *Closure* 38
Bardo State Awareness in Treating Adolescents 38
Bardo State Awareness in Treating the Elderly 40

CHAPTER 4 Using Grief Stages in Group Psychotherapy 43
Grief Stages in an Addiction Support Group 43
The Role of the Grief Process in Addiction Counseling 45

CHAPTER 5 Using Grief Stages in Addiction Treatment 49
Treatment of Chemical Dependency 49
Treatment of Other Addictions 52

CHAPTER 6 A Lecture on Grief Anniversaries 54
Introduction 54
The Lecture 54
Following the Lecture 56
The Risks in Ignoring Grief Anniversaries 57

CHAPTER 7 What the 12 Steps Say about Grief 58
The History of the 12 Steps 58
The 12 Steps 59

CHAPTER 8 On Beyond the Grief Stages 64
Contrasting the Medicine of the West and the East 64
The Buddhist Concept of *Between* States (*Bardo* States) 66
Incorporating Awareness of *Between* States in Western Psychotherapy 68
Treatment Modalities for Exploring *Between* States in Therapy 70
Awaited: "The True Nature of Reality" Therapy 75

CHAPTER 9 Existential Therapy 76

CHAPTER 10 Collapsing the *Bardo* States 79
Responses to Painful *Bardo* States 80
Mindfulness to Collapse a *Bardo* State 82
Forgiveness to Collapse a *Bardo* State 84

Taking Direct Action to Collapse a *Bardo* State	88
Terrorism Viewed As Action to Collapse a *Bardo* State	91
Taking Sides to Collapse a *Bardo* State	92
Dreams and Reality	93
Being Too Hasty in Collapsing a *Bardo* State	95
Foot-Dragging in Collapsing a *Bardo* State	97
CHAPTER 11 The Rewards of *Bardo* Knowledge	99
Clarification of Life's Priorities	99
Understanding Impermanence As Promise	100
Greater Awareness of Living	101
Acceptance of Physical Death	101
Recognition That Impermanence Is Normal	101
Living in the "Now"	102
Epilogue	103
Bibliography	105

PREFACE

In the last episode of *The Waves*, by Virginia Woolf, a "phrase maker" named Bernard looks back on his sixty years and sums up what he knows about the other characters and what he's learned about life.

As a phrase maker who is now the same age as Bernard, I've put in the pages of *The Reality Between* a summary of what I know about grief, psychotherapy, addiction, physics, and Eastern thought. They all converge, I have discovered, at what Buddhists call The Truth of Impermanence.

Whether you are a provider or a consumer of mental and behavioral health services, I believe that you will come away from the first reading of this book with the sobering notion that we are, on the whole, a brittle people. The purpose of this book is to show how we can discard this brittleness and learn to sway gently and safely with the winds of change.

As a licensed substance abuse counselor and psychotherapist, I have witnessed many hundreds of therapists diagnose as "stress" the dozens of painful, life-altering changes presented by their patients. I submit in this book that what the patients are experiencing is not stress but grief, in the truest and greatest sense of the word. The reason most therapists don't recognize grief is that they have been conditioned to associate grief only with bereavement. In addition, no therapist has ever taken a class (or done a clinical rotation) called, "The Ephemeral Nature of Life."

In my first book, *Outwitting Your Alcoholic*, I explored the nature of addiction and lightly touched on the role of grief in the addiction process. *The Reality Between*, however, gives me an opportunity to greatly expand on how our lives are dominated by constant change and loss. This means, of course, that we are always in a grief process. But the good news is that a process is a steady march toward eventual resolution, which can be accelerated if one truly accepts that life is one long chain of hellos and goodbyes. My careful study of Buddhist practice over the last twenty years and my attendance in 1993 at a week-long retreat with the Dalai Lama of Tibet in Tucson, Arizona, taught me about impermanence and led indirectly to this book.

Chapter 1 of *The Reality Between* explores why we don't see (or don't want to see) The Truth of Impermanence. It also provides a checklist that will begin to give the reader a sense of how many states of change he or she may be going through every second. Chapters 2–4 show how various models of grieving came to be and how grief is greatly underdiagnosed by Western psychotherapists. Chapters 5–7 detail how recovering addicts can benefit from what Freud called "griefwork." Chapters 8–11 take Western griefwork into Eastern thought to show the ubiquity of grief and how it can be successfully treated if therapists learn to see grief stages as change states that give life its "sizzle."

I would like to thank my patients and clients for teaching me what I know about psychotherapy and the magic of recovery. Elizabeth Welsh put this book in its final form; this is, indeed, her gift to all of us and is very much appreciated. And as always, I would also like to thank Pat Kenny for her keen design and photography talents and for helping this old phrase maker stand at the *bardo of possibility*.

INTRODUCTION

What if Elisabeth Kübler-Ross was right?

As psychotherapists, we understand that a person copes with grief through a well-defined process that starts with denial and isolation, then moves on to anger, bargaining, depression, and, with diligence, into acceptance. We understand this when a patient speaks to us of mourning; we take the bereaved through Kübler-Ross's grief stages, ask them to write a letter to their dead, and perhaps release to the heavens a helium-filled balloon or two. Figuratively dusting off our hands and making a note in the patient chart, we return to our offices with the illusion that we made things better.

But what if Kübler-Ross—the leading thanatologist of our time and the founder of the modern hospice movement—was even more right than we thought?

What if she made a huge mistake by cloaking her now famous grief remedy in the mantle of death? What if psychotherapists are missing a great opportunity to bring their patients closer to healing, and themselves closer to enlightenment, by their failure to pick up on what Kübler-Ross seemed to imply in her seminal work, *On Death and Dying*? Namely, that grief is the common denominator of life—that every event, from the largest to the smallest, involves change; change means loss, and loss means grief. What if Western therapists began to see life, as Eastern practitioners do, as always impermanent, always in flux, always in change, and abounding in small, large, and devastating grief stages, most of which are not known because they are not looked for?

Or let's put it this way. When we see a patient in a "one-on-one" or a group setting and hear him speak of the death of a loved one or the loss of a key relationship, we don't think twice about reaching up on the shelf and pulling down one of Kübler-Ross's many books. But when we hear of seemingly smaller non-death issues, such as empty-nest syndrome, aging, graduation, marriage, divorce, retirement, job change, change in social identity, ill health, or even addiction, do we see these as involving grief stages? If not, we fail to see our patients acting out their lives through *time,* Einstein's fourth dimension. Time that has as its central feature The Buddhist Truth of *Impermanence*.

Alas, it seems that Kübler-Ross never said that denial-isolation, anger, bargaining, and depression *weren't* stand-alone issues. We just assume she did, because she presented them in the context of the ultimate loss—physical death. Because we relate Kübler-Ross to death, when we see patients who are angry, depressed, and bargaining, we fail to see these issues in the patient's "grief context." We never look for (or know to look for) the grief context that is always present. This grief context can range in importance from huge to tiny, from paramount to picayune, but if we work hard enough, we'll find it. That is, if we accept the fact that it's there.

Grief must be placed into a larger, more universal, more Eastern context. If it is, the practitioner will see that when patients speak of emotional pain, they are speaking of grief. When patients speak of confusion, they are speaking of losses that the therapist must strain to hear. When they speak of addiction to mood-altering substances (whether they pour them down their throats or summon them by high-risk activities), they are medicating grief. Once therapists come to understand that every encounter with a patient is about grief, seen or unseen, noticed or ignored, they will go a long way toward empowering their patients to see their lives as ever-changing, ever-streaming, and ever-flowing with hellos and goodbyes. And they'll go further toward their long-held goal of being true, compassionate healers.

This book explores what it means to put *time* back into psychotherapy. Certainly most therapists understand and console their clients with phrases like, "This, too, shall pass," or "This won't go away overnight." But to truly understand the grief context of a patient is to come to grips with the notion that a major feature of time is *impermanence*. Accordingly, we'll explore Kübler-Ross's "Five Stages of Grief" and see how they can be understood as "Five Stages of Change." I will explain how dying in the middle of these grief stages (which most people do) is virtually guaranteed to send a person to the spirit world in denial, anger, or depression. The history of grief treatment will be explored, and I will show how the Kübler-Ross grief stages may also be used with non-death griefs such as addiction. I will then discuss life changes as "states of *between*" or "*bardo* states" (as Eastern practitioners do) and will show therapists how to be aware of all the minor and major grief stages a client is throwing at them. In other words, this book will show how Kübler-Ross got it right the first time—she just didn't go far enough.

If I can convey to the reader the notion that The Truth of Impermanence gives life its "juice," I will have earned my keep and reinforced my long-held notion that the meaning of life is death, and the meaning of death is life.

1

Our Flight from The Truth of Impermanence

All those snow boots, way too small; left behind, goodbye.

—Ian Tyson, *Lost Herd*

We live in a universe wherein there is no permanence. There may seem to be permanence, but that is an illusion. No one likes this situation, so we pretend that there *is* permanence by establishing daily routines and living lives dominated by habits and rituals—backing our cars out of the driveway; telling our loved ones, "I'll see you tonight"; taking pleasure in a baby's first steps or words; carving memorials in granite; and assuming that we will be remembered after we die. We deal with impermanence by attempting to hang onto people, places, things, money, property, and prestige. We congratulate ourselves for having children and grandchildren (and/or for writing books) that will keep us remembered for at least the next three or four decades. After that, it all gets fuzzy.

Unsettling *Between* States and Ever-Present Change

We don't like it that we are perpetually living life in unsettling and unappealing *between* states, yet these states are always with us. Most often, we don't perceive that we are in them because we cannot see or otherwise experience infinitesimal changes such as flowers blooming or entire continents in motion. We can see time neither in slow motion nor fast motion, and our busy schedules and denial systems take care of the rest. We view vast glaciers and large boulders as solid, though in fact they are more-or-less fluid. We don't notice this because our lifespans are short compared with theirs. If we were able to see otherwise, they would appear to be flowing and changing like rivers.

The process of disintegration starts the moment that something comes into existence in this world, whether it's a subatomic particle, a flower, a bird—or us. That's because impermanence is built into the system, just as a new car automatically depreciates the moment it is driven off the sales lot. In other words, the seeds of our own demise are contained within us. Most death-producing illnesses, in fact, lie hidden inside us until some unseen bell goes "bong." This ever-present change can be seen as a negative—or as a phenomenon that is dynamic, crackling, and juiced with possibilities.

During the last hours of the old millennium, many of us saw a newspaper article in which it was pointed out that in the Grand Canyon of Arizona, a hiker heading toward the Colorado River (a mile below the canyon rim) passes the equivalent of 120 millennia (120,000 years) with each step she takes! That's one-thirtieth of an inch for every thousand years—sobering and staggering figures that speak to us of time rushing onward.

Why We Don't Acknowledge Impermanence

Almost all of us go through our developmental stages (infancy, adolescence, youth, middle age, and old age) turning a blind eye to the fact that we are ephemeral—that future generations, that is to say *near* future generations, will never know we existed. There are many reasons we can't (or don't want to) recognize our impermanence.

Change May Not Be Readily Perceptible. First, the flow of time from the past toward the future moves us imperceptibly toward change. Yesterday flows into today, which will soon flow into tomorrow. Childhood streams into youth, and then middle age dominates until old age takes us toward death. In nature, the seasons sweep by from hot to cold and then back again. We certainly notice that it's snowing outside where not long ago intense heat dominated, but in the span of a day, we never perceive this seasonal dance. Likewise, we note at times that it is getting lighter earlier in the day, and we may congratulate ourselves for knowing that it's because Earth rotates on its axis, but we hardly notice the rotation, so deep we are into our daily activities.

Religions Promise Life after Death. Second, many religions promise that Heaven awaits those of faith—so why worry about impermanence? With the idea that eternal bliss is our goal, the issue of impermanence seems a thought not worth entertaining. Buddhists believe in reincarnation and suggest that a more fortunate rebirth can be had by those who work with an experienced teacher and meditate on the power of the inner mind. But why try to bend that mind around impossible-to-understand notions such as impermanence if we are right down the street from Nirvana?

Contemplating impermanence is not at odds with spiritual or religious beliefs, however. Acknowledging that death is a certainty may provide the intensity or vitality needed to expand our spiritual horizons. Indeed, a person whose spiritual practice allows him or her to become more comfortable with the inevitability of death may become even more focused on spirituality with the realization that every moment counts. Rather than resulting in passivity, resignation, or morbidity, The Truth of Impermanence should launch us all toward greater diligence in our spiritual practice. It certainly has done so for the Hindus.

The ultimate reality of Hinduism is called *Brahman*, the omnipresent, infinite, incomprehensible, inner essence of all things. The manifestation of Brahman in the human soul is called *Atman*. Hindus see one manifestation of Brahman as Shiva, the cosmic dancer who is the god of creation and destruction. Another manifestation of Brahman, the god Vishnu, is the preserver of the universe, which in Hinduism is rhythmic, fluid, and ever-changing. It is Vishnu who appears as Krishna and dialogues with the warrior Arjuna on a field of battle in the *Bhagavad Gita*. Thus we see that Hindus are comfortable with creation and destruction to the degree that it's central to their beliefs.

Perceived Danger Immobilizes Us. Third, we resist delving into The Truth of Impermanence because, like most animals, we are biologically conditioned to become rigid when facing danger. We're all familiar with the term, "deer-in-the-headlights look," which so aptly describes how animals appear when startled by a fast-approaching car. It's also how human beings (who are animals, as well) look and act when they encounter the death of the second, of the minute, of the hour, of the day, of the month, of the decades, of the years. Shall we take a close look at how ephemeral we are? No, thanks; we'd rather watch television to see how fast the newest celebrity is achieving superstardom and other dead ends.

Yet humans are somehow, at some subconscious level, aware that change is all about them; that life is fluid and dynamic. We're fond of such sayings as, "The more things change, the more they stay the same." We read knowingly about plate tectonics, how Europe was once over here and now India is over there. We glance at a newspaper story that shows how Earth's moon may have been a chunk of blown-off planet we captured millions of years ago—but what of it? How does this affect our mortgages and the fact that we have kids to raise? Despite this, the more adventurous of us, the more enlightened of us, come to be at ease with the notion that an individual human is like one atom in a single cluster of trillion-star galaxies.

Ironically, however, most of us deal with life's fluidity with rigidity, which inevitably leads to problems and stresses. The answer is to reach a deeper understanding, through a spiritual master or a trained psychotherapist, that to be fully alive, we need to become, in our outlook and in our perception of reality, *just as fluid and dynamic as the ever-changing world around us.* Only though constant communion with change can we stay spiritually flexible and emotionally agile.

Denial of Death May Be "Hard Wired." Fourth, we balk at the contemplation of impermanence because we're simply not built to do so. It's odd to think that our survival as a species may have depended upon how well we could ignore time and The Truth of Impermanence. But perhaps our ancestors, millions of years ago, survived to breed because they weren't concerned in the least about philosophical thought. Perhaps our forebears were the fittest for survival because they took quickly to illusion. While others of a more philosophical bent were being trampled by mastodons, our ancestors, strangers to The Truth of Impermanence, survived to produce offspring because they cared not a whit for imponderables.

Indeed, the psychologist Ernest Becker wrote that the denial of death (not reproduction and not the quest for food or shelter) is the fundamental human drive. If that is so, then it's clear that our very survival as a species places a terrifically high premium on how successfully we turn a blind eye to our own mortality; consequently, the comprehension of impermanence is a task for which we are neurologically ill prepared. When we are called upon today to make routine decisions (at home, in the workplace, or anywhere else), we rapidly scan our brains for past experiences, attempt to sort out potential pros and cons, dodge subconscious fears, and try to integrate everything quickly into a coherent thought that will serve as an answer. We are adept at solving our pressing problems, but we continue to live in illusion—perhaps the ultimate price we pay for survival.

There's no shame in that. We can't fault ourselves for not knowing *how* we got here or *why* we're here. We need assume no guilt for being too busy with survival to look closely at the true nature of reality. We can't be blamed for not noticing that every subatomic event, according to the physics books, is marked by the annihilation of the initial particles and the creation of new ones. We're too busy feeding our kids, pleasing our supervisors, and watching the performance of our 401(k) plans. However, it is possible to begin to make friends with impermanence and do the best job we can. The irony that our instinct for survival makes us insensitive to the ultimate nature of reality doesn't mean we can't try to importune it.

While it might take a Buddhist master to truly comprehend The Truth of Impermanence, we can at least call it by its name and acknowledge that it's there, though extremely hard to see. Just because we can't understand the nature of God, a "higher power," the Buddha Nature, or Allah, that doesn't mean we should stop believing in it or cease our efforts to contact a "power greater" through prayer or some other intercession.

We Refuse to Explore the Unknowable. Fifth, we shun thinking about the unknowable because we're convinced that it *is* unknowable and that an effort to grasp it is doomed to failure. Nathaniel Branden, author of *The Six Pillars of Self-Esteem*, wrote:

> If we face the basic problems of life with an attitude of "Who am I to know? Who am I to judge? Who am I to decide?"—or "It is dangerous to be conscious"—or "It is futile to try to think or understand"—we are undercut at the outset. A mind does not struggle for that which it regards as impossible or undesirable.

What Branden seems to be saying is that when we encounter a difficult-to-fathom notion such as The Truth of Impermanence, we prejudge it to be ineffable and of little use to our lives. In so doing, we shrink from self-conscious mortality, we continue to wander in the illusion of permanence, and we arrive at another self-fulfilling prophecy.

We Fear Uncomfortable Truths. Sixth, we may simply be afraid. It's not easy or natural to look behind the curtain of life; to desire a deeper seeing of the ephemeral nature of our existence. For one thing, it might collapse the fragile ego state that keeps us going. We seem to be under the impression that if we don't peer too closely at our lives, we'll be okay. If we can make it to hospice care before ever encountering an awareness of death, we win some sort of prize. We figure we've beaten the system if we successfully bury our heads in work and pleasure and never learn that the ancient Asians visualized the briefness of life as a speeding chariot viewed through a chink in the wall; if we never acknowledge to ourselves that, in the words of Irish playwright Samuel Beckett, "we're born on the edge of a grave."

Others of us may regard the study of impermanence as nihilism—belief that life has no apparent meaning; that creation is devoid of any plan set in motion by anything other than Richard Dawkins's blind watchmaker. In other words, we're afraid that any deity we worship will admonish us for taking too close a look at the cogs and flywheels that make the whole system work. Better to hold onto the illusion of an afterlife than to risk it all by importuning The Truth of Impermanence.

We Avoid Taking Responsibility for Our Suffering. Seventh, we hide The Truth of Impermanence up on the top shelf behind the crackers because as long as we can keep this troubling reality out of sight, we don't have to take responsibility for our actions. As long as we can stay in delusion, we can tell ourselves that others are causing our suffering. In actuality, our suffering is *caused* by our delusions. Said another way, our fundamental ignorance of reality leads to delusions, and these delusions cause suffering. Only by giving it a name can we avoid this. Only by understanding The Truth of Impermanence at a deep, conscious level can we know that our time on Earth is transitory—extremely transitory, at that. Out of this awareness, keen insight into life's possibilities suddenly becomes available. We stop blaming others for the suffering in our lives and live in freedom and responsibility.

Western Medicine Encourages Our Illusions. Eighth, we turn our backs on impermanence because modern medicine—that is to say, *Western* medicine—asks us to. Or perhaps it's more honest to say that we demand of Western medicine that it cushion us from the reality of death. There's no argument that medical science has brought us great benefits. Today's child is likely to live into her nineties—unthinkable a century ago, when life expectancy was half that. But that great success comes with a price: As modern medicine holds out the brass ring of an extended lifespan, we grab at that ring as if it can spare us from death. Surely we don't need to think about end-of-life issues if doctors can keep us alive and religions can extend us into eternity (a word a physicist would never utter). Are we then simply extending our lifelong state of *between* (or *bardo* state) without thinking about what it actually means? If we fail to discover (not invent) its meaning, an extended life holds but a hollow promise.

We grasp at everything a physician offers to gain valuable weeks before life's exit. Unless we involve hospice care or prepare advance directives, we will likely die far from home, tangled in a spider's web of wires, tubes, and wheezing life-support machines. Forgetting that medicine's job is to offer better health, we come to think of it as a guarantor of longer life. We demand that Western medicine continuously do battle with Nature, but Nature knows that it's the job of every person to eventually die so that life can be perpetuated.

If you push against the skin of your head, your chest, your arms, or your legs, you will feel a slight give. Press harder, and you will reach a painful point where you cannot press further. This is where your bones are. Remove your skin and your muscles and you'll find a skeleton. This skeleton represents impermanence, and our skin and muscles represent the illusion we clutch to keep the skeleton hidden. Only when we acknowledge the presence of the bone beneath our soft tissues can we do an adequate job of understanding that we have a finite period of time on Earth. Modern medicine can only do so much to keep the skin on the bone, yet we continue to ask it to push Nature to the degree that many of us go into the death process both reluctantly and with a keen sense of failure. Failure? Since when is a phenomenon as natural as death a failure? Isn't that the way it's supposed to be? Aren't we supposed to die so that life can continue? Doesn't the inevitability of death underscore how important it is to live well? Our obsession with how long we live gets in the way of how *well* we live.

And it's not fair to lay all the blame for our fear of death on modern medicine. One has only to witness the proliferation of cryogenic facilities that take our fears of impermanence to extremes. In 2002, baseball legend Ted Williams died. Ordinarily, he would have been either embalmed or cremated, but his son had other ideas. He delivered his father's body to a cryogenics firm in Scottsdale, Arizona, where the great hitter's head was separated and his body was suspended upside down in a frozen state. Nearby in this cold, vertical graveyard are many others who are slated to be thawed and reanimated in a future world where some anticipate that technology will make this possible. This macabre response to death cannot be seen as simply pushing Nature the way modern medicine does. This is far beyond pushing; it's a ludicrous attempt to stick our heads in the sand even after death has occurred, and those who take part in it are pushing death anxiety to pathological extremes.

The Essence of Humanness Is Unclear. Ninth, we fear impermanence because, to paraphrase the daughter of Shakespeare's King Lear, we have "ever but slenderly known ourselves." In other words, we really don't know who we are. And if we don't know who we are, we can't face death and the many other states of *between* that surround us. So who are we, anyway? For hundreds of years, scientists, philosophers, and clerics have pondered this question. Are humans more than their arms and legs, eyes and noses? If all our appendages were removed, would we still be human? Does our humanness lie in the cerebral cortex, or in our older mammalian/reptilian brains? or all in combination? Does our humanness reside in what is thought of as our soul? Is our humanness based on carefully crafted props and "things" that define us: our given names, our social security numbers, our office nameplates, our resumes, our credit cards, and our material possessions, like the sports car we drive, or the fact that our name is carved on a heavy granite memorial somewhere? When such diseases as Alzheimer's strike and remove our memories while preserving our heartbeats, are we still individuals? Take all this away, along with all the meaningless things we do to consume time, and who is left? Is it us? So, who *is* "us"?

We eschew insight into our inner natures and continue to prop up the illusion that we are here—solid, stable, and forever—that is, until death and all its *bardo* state henchmen collapse our carefully crafted illusions. We then become extremely uncomfortable and search for mood-altering drugs, television, relationships, pornography, gambling, compulsive exercise, shopping, work, and Internet chat rooms to medicate the sudden loss of an illusion that has collapsed like a mobile home in the path of a Category 5 hurricane. Having no knowledge of a deeper reality—the reality of impermanence—we wrestle with this loss until someone notices that we seem depressed, and onto antidepressants we go.

Our Society Idolizes Youth. Tenth and last, we ignore our impermanence because our society is geared toward the celebration of youth. This was not always the case. Back when cultures and societies depended on the graybeards to show them the way to survival, older members of society were revered. When we seasonally migrated to hunting and fishing grounds, they were the ones who knew the way. Without their wisdom, we became lost, and being lost all too often meant death. Today, however, we tend to think that older heads have little to offer us. This is buttressed by marketing studies telling us that those in the sixty-plus age group spend very little on music, movies, and trendy clothing; therefore, as a demographic, they disappear from the radar screen. And in modern-day America, we tend not to remember or respect a demographic niche that doesn't freely waste its disposable income.

Persistent Evidence of Impermanence

Impermanence, insistent truth that it is, doesn't stay hidden forever. Change gets "in our face" when we notice the growing collection of our children's outgrown toys and baby clothes, and when we see how threadbare and out-of-style our own clothing has become. As children, we become excited about growing older because it brings us the promise of freedom and the ability to do "big kid" or adult things. Young children notice that the older they get, the more freedom is available. We may be allowed to cross the street alone, or no longer need a babysitter. We glance in the mirror and see that it's time to begin shaving, or that we're finally taller than our parents.

The further passage of time allows us to meet friends at the mall, and soon a car becomes ours. This leads to dating, which leads to children. We often get out of denial at thirty when we begin to realize that we are mortal after all, and that someday we will become older and die. But that's a long way off, we tell ourselves, so why think of it now?

Older people find signs of aging in the mirror; we term the wrinkles "laugh lines" and joke that being bald and gray at the temples is sexy. The hand that sticks out of our shirtsleeve startles us in middle age because it is the hand, complete with age spots and tiny creases, that once belonged to a cherished but long-dead parent.

Thus we raise our children and grandchildren, all the while noticing that our bodies are becoming physically ravaged and that we need to get those nips and tucks from cosmetic surgeons. Then we make our first acquaintance with the Botox syringe. As we start receiving those AARP cards in the mail and getting those retirement parties, we understand, on some level at least, that death awaits us. But why think of it now—we've got ocean cruises to take and grandchildren to play with. So the final impermanence, the greatest change of all, becomes ignored so diligently that even making choices about cemetery plots or deciding whether or not to be cremated is deferred until it's too late.

We notice that the morning newspaper covers the same tired issues that mesmerized us forty years ago. We no longer linger over the style section and are forced to admit that we fail to recognize the young, strangely dressed people on the celebrity page. New movies seem to feature threadbare plots tied to special effects that are both fantastic and noisy. Finally, we must come to acknowledge that one after another, our friends and acquaintances are dying off and that we're attending far more funerals than we once did. Indeed, we notice that we no longer turn to the society column to keep track of those we know—we turn to the obituary page.

Our lives consist of waiting, anxiety, dread, impatience, and fear, yet we can't allow ourselves to admit The Truth of Impermanence or to admit that we're merely passing through; merely loitering on Earth, like the billions who came before us. And barring collision with a large comet or a nuclear exchange between superpowers, untold billions will succeed us. Looking at old family portraits found in the attic or at an antique shop, we gaze at stern-looking, rough, bonneted and bearded faces and find ourselves knowing, on some deep level, that all those in the photographs, including the babies, have long since departed, populating cemeteries both quaint and forgotten. And so, perhaps, have their children and their children's children.

Our denial systems are jarred by the deaths of friends, family, loved ones, and finally, of ourselves. We grieve, but we continue to deny that life is all about tiny, big, and humongous changes. We know they're there, but it's like that carton of milk that we subconsciously know we need from the supermarket but can't bring ourselves to call to mind. Yet we cannot escape, try as we might, the fact that something is born and dies in us every second. Ultimately, we will die, Earth will die, our solar system will die, the Milky Way galaxy will die, and our universe will die.

In folly, we take solace in transitory things such as material goods (cars, homes, and clothing), technical innovations, and cosmetic fads that foolishly allow us to think that happiness will forever be ours. Television programs and movies persuade us that we need these things, and that with them, we can medicate what's bothering us. Got some depression? Go shopping. Feeling stressed? Have a martini. Afraid of death? Start accumulating worldly goods so that you can delude yourself into thinking that with so much debt, you will never die.

But close examination reveals that change and death are all around us—if we just choose to see it. Science programs on television tell us that the body builds and repairs billions of new cells every minute and that our hair grows so many millimeters per day. We look outside and notice flowers opening and closing, the sun sets and then rises, the dew burns off and re-forms, trees drop their leaves in the fall and get them back in spring, and clouds hurtle to and fro. This cyclic existence is what we call progress. We love the freshness and the possibility it provides, but we don't care for the fact that we're part of this death-rebirth cycle. That's when it gets personal, that's why we deny it exists, that's why we avert our eyes, and that's when our fears develop.

The Price We Pay for Denial

Turning our backs on the true nature of reality has a reward, but at a terrible price. The *reward* is that we can blissfully float along in life, secure in our illusion that impermanence can be easily dealt with by one more martini or one more gaily lit distraction. The *price* that we pay for ignoring reality usually comes at the end of our lives. Just as a person falling from an airplane without a parachute finds it problematic only in the final second of an otherwise scenic freefall, human beings find that the penalty they pay for ignoring impermanence means a lonely hospital bed occupied by a terrified, terminally ill person who wishes he or she had packed a little more thoughtfully, and a little earlier, for the trip.

During late summer when hurricanes approach, the Weather Channel shows us hundreds of people boarding up their homes and retreating to higher ground. They were forewarned by meteorologists, whose expertise is to predict these great storms. This seems logical to us. Indeed, we would think it the height of folly to see someone going about everyday life in the face of a huge hurricane as if nothing were about to happen. But this is how we in the West act, even though we know for absolute certainty that the biggest storm of all (death)—the one that is guaranteed to do to us the ultimate physical damage—is that terrible black cloud right over the horizon.

When we finally start thinking about death, it's often when we receive bad news from the doctor. Trembling and confused, we start lashing out (with plenty of anger freely available to all). And why wouldn't we? We've spent our entire lives as if death were a stranger. We've lived for eighty years (with the exception of the last month) as if death were a foreign concept. If we do the math, we find that one month is only 0.1% of 80 years. In this extremely short *bardo* state, we must go through the grief stages—and we certainly don't have much time for it. When we lose a friend, we at least have a few months or years to process the loss. But if we've postponed thoughts of our own death, it forces us to go through stages of grief in a trice. When time runs out, is it any wonder, then, that we barely have enough time to get out of the denial-isolation stage and into the depression and anger stages (to use the Kübler-Ross model)? It seems we'd benefit by processing the grief stages as early as possible so we don't die in the middle of them. Dying when we're angry is the price we pay for expiring *in medias res* of the grief process.

In fact, so many among us die depressed and angry that one is tempted to believe that this is what death looks like—what death *must* look like. We see our parents and grandparents struggling through anger and depression during their final days to the degree that we are tempted to think that dying while in a state of fear and total bewilderment is the norm. It certainly doesn't need to be. And perhaps watching people struggle prior to their imminent death scares us all the more and launches us into a downward spiral in which the more fearful we get, the more fearful we get, and then we become even more fearful…

Embracing The Truth of Impermanence

It certainly isn't necessary for us to become overwhelmed by The Truth of Impermanence. It can be successfully argued that it has very little to do with our workaday world, in which coffee needs to be made, the kids need rousting out of bed, jobs needs to get done, and an evening round of cards or television finishes off the day. However, impermanence may at least be acknowledged and accepted. Mindfulness and meditation are good places to start. And why just *accept* The Truth of Impermanence when you can *embrace* it for the fullness it provides?

An easy-to-understand analogy illustrates how humans can deal with illusions such as impermanence. The illusion of *solidity*, for instance. That chair you're sitting on may feel solid to you, but in fact, it's not. Quite the opposite is true. It's mostly vast reaches of empty space. It's made of atoms, which consist of negatively charged electrons whizzing near the speed of light around a positively charged nucleus. It has been estimated that if a single atom were a fourteen-story building, the atom's nucleus would be the size of a grain of sand. Described a different way, the volume of an atom is more than a trillion times the volume of its nucleus. If you could *see* your chair the way it actually is, it would look like a typical night sky, only with atoms sparsely scattered here and there rather than stars. Yet your chair holds you because certain nuclear forces prevent electrons from spiraling into the nuclei. When a few gazillion of these nearly empty space balls are formed into a chair, you sit in it, write your letters, and have coffee with a friend, always under the illusion that what you're sitting on is solid. Certainly, importuning The Truth of Impermanence is far more important to our lives than teasing *solidity* from illusion, but the chair analogy is useful.

Physics, the study of motion, time, and energy, has long shown us that the world we live in—the world we try to ignore—is alive with the dance of creation and destruction. In *The Dancing Wu Li Masters,* Gary Zukav wrote that the world is a "sparkling realm of continual creation, transformation and annihilation." And don't be misled into thinking that this creation and annihilation stuff is simply what subatomic particles go through. No, these subatomic particles, which are the building blocks of everything—including you and me—*are the dance itself.* Most physicists today don't think of particles as "things" so much as condensations or concentrations of energy that come and go; they shy away from describing the structure of *things* in favor of describing the structure of *movement*.

How interesting that Western scientists like Albert Einstein have been extremely good at intuiting the relativity of time, yet Western psychotherapists have virtually ignored time for more than a hundred years. It's as if we in the West are adept in defining, delineating, measuring, and quantifying time, but when it comes to our daily lives, we deny that it affects us.

Let's try it this way: If we can't seem to get around impermanence, let's try to imagine a world where *permanence* reigns. If our universe was characterized by permanence, the Big Bang would never have happened, hydrogen atoms would never have been created, the galaxies would never have constellated their trillions of stars and started their lazy rotations, the planets would be AWOL, our solar system would be but a dream, Earth in all its blue beauty would never have gotten off the drawing board, and we would wouldn't be around to think such weird thoughts. There would be no such thing as transpiration, metabolism, DNA, photosynthesis, development, or maturation, and certainly, a laptop computer battery that lasts longer than two hours would be out of the cosmic question. There may be a world where there is true solidity, where non-change dominates—a world where there are no *between* or *bardo* states—but if so, it's not in this universe. Alas, we are stuck with a world wherein change is the controlling factor; there's no alternative, so we must tip our collective hats to it.

Recognizing the Centrality of *Between* States

The following exercise will bring the nature of reality one step closer. Take out a legal pad and start two columns: one headed "Acute *Bardo* States" and the other headed "Chronic *Bardo* States." (In Tibetan, *bar* means "in between" and *do* means "suspended." It is often written *bar-do*.) In the "Acute" column, write down the *bardo* states that most often rise to the level of your consciousness and might require talk therapy and/or medication to resolve. In the "Chronic" column, list the *bardo* states that don't always rise to the level of consciousness and that, unless they are rendering you depressed or anxious, may not require professional help. The kinds of lists you might generate are shown on the next page, along with a third list of additional *between* states.

When you're done, you'll see that at any given time, you are in a very large number of *between* states. Indeed, you'll probably be staggered by the dozens of transitional states that stare back at you from the legal pad, because most of us have little idea of how many states of *between* we are experiencing at any given moment. These *bardo* states should not all be thought of as deterministic or as driving us and restricting our choices (the way Sigmund Freud said that repression, unconscious forces, irrational drives, and past events drove his patients). Nor should these *bardo* states be thought of as disease or sickness. But this huge list of change states demonstrates that impermanence can be regarded as the single most pervasive, most insistent, and most constant influence upon human beings. Yet we in the West not only don't recognize that fact, we work hard to preserve the illusion that everything stays more-or-less the same.

Examples of Acute *Bardo* States	Examples of Chronic *Bardo* States
(Acute *bardo* states rise to the level of consciousness and often require talk therapy or medication)	(Chronic *bardo* states don't always rise to the level of consciousness and may not require professional help)
Loss of a loved one to physical death	Aging
Divorce and other forms of separation	Developmental stages (infancy, puberty, etc.)
Trauma such as theft, burglary, murder, terrorist acts	Travel that is longer than a daily commute to work
Waiting for the results of a medical test	Empty-nest syndrome
Driving to work	Transitioning from being a young health care provider to an elderly health care consumer
Impatience at the store check-out counter	
Being on a diet	
Falling asleep	Extended psychotherapy
Dream states	Summer vacation
Becoming awake	Emotional or physical abandonment during childhood
Involvement in legal action	
Bidding on a house	Diasporas (such as the 40-year Israeli exodus from Egypt and the current exile of Tibetans to India)
Major illness	
Addiction relapse	
Attending the death of a loved one	Chronic illness
Major power outages	Ignorance (delusion)
Joblessness	Restlessness between projects
Killing time at Starbucks between appointments	Extended joblessness
	Substance abuse
Stoplights and heavy traffic	Existential angst
Waiting for the dentist	General restlessness
	Writing a book
	Probation
	Menopause
	Generalized anxiety
	Mild depression such as dysthymia or dysphoria
	Perceived coarsening of manners by those around you
	Loss of quality of life where you live

Examples of Other *Between* States

Transitioning from...

sickness to health	disconnection to connection
helplessness to choices	isolation to community
"can't" to "can"	chaos to harmony
subconscious to conscious	invisible to visible
enslavement to liberation	violence to peace
confusion to clarity	egoism to compassion
ignorance to knowledge	autism to outreach
blindness to vision	repression to disclosure
disdain to respect	hopelessness to hope
complication to simplicity	insecurity to security
hubris to humility	fragmentation to congruence
addiction to recovery	insanity to sanity
seen to unseen	bewilderment to insight
shame to self-esteem	negative to positive
apathy to values	incredulity to faith

2

The Rise of Grief Models

> *They do not understand that I have to effect different transitions; have to cover the entrances and exits of several different men who alternately act their parts as Bernard.*
>
> —Virginia Woolf, *The Waves*

Although most Western therapists do not yet see grief and the grief process as states of *between* (unlike their Eastern counterparts), such states do have a great role to play in Western psychotherapy. Without question, grief is the closest thing to a *between* state that therapists in the West acknowledge. It's where we recognize a change state, though we do not notice that it's merely one of hundreds of change states we go through every day.

Thanks to a few devoted writers and researchers, the grief process is now a well-accepted philosophy and therapeutic technique, but most psychologists and psychotherapists pay attention to grief only after the occurrence of a physical death or the loss of a close relationship. Once this grief has been processed and the griever comes to understand that his lost loved one remains with him in a much different relationship, he feels better, the pain dissipates, and he and his therapist will get on with their lives completely unaware that there were hundreds of other *between* states they blithely missed. The word *grief*, incidentally, comes from the Middle English word *gref* and the Old French words *gref* and *greave*. It means, literally, *heavy*, *grave*, *difficult*, and *troubled*.

Buddhism's View of Grief

The Buddha probably didn't have grief in mind when he realized his Four Noble Truths over 2,500 years ago, but the Awakened One did teach that attachments (and other bad habits) lead directly to suffering. Because he saw that attachments bring suffering, he taught that humans should avoid them if they wish to avoid suffering *(dukka)*. Easily said, but not easily done. He taught that suffering does exist (Truth 1) and that attachments are one of the biggest sources of suffering (Truth 2). He further taught that detachment trumps *samsara*, the endless cycle of suffering (Truth 3), and that we may keep attachment at bay by traveling the Eightfold Path (Truth 4).

What the Buddha seemed to be implying was that grief is the price we pay for love and desire. If we choose to love, we expose ourselves to pain. Ask any adolescent who's had his or her heart broken for the first time. Ask anyone at a funeral who deeply mourns the passing of a loved one. In any new relationship we embark upon, the Buddha warns, whether it's a spouse or a new pet, we say "hello" knowing that someday we will say "goodbye." So it's best, perhaps, not to say hello. So imbued with this knowledge was the Buddha that upon his death, he was said to have comforted his followers with these words: "Decay is inherent in all compounded things. Strive on with diligence."

The Truth of Impermanence is not exactly a central tenet of Buddhism; it's more accurate to say that Buddhism *begins* and *ends* with impermanence—that impermanence is contained in Buddhism, and Buddhism is contained in impermanence. The Buddha taught that our suffering on Earth stems primarily from our desire to grasp at people, clutch our situations, and hoard our experiences, rather than allowing them to flow in and out of our lives as the fluid, transitory phenomena they truly are. The mystical poet William Blake caught this spirit well when he wrote:

> He who binds himself to a joy,
> Does the winged life destroy;
> But he who kisses the Joy as it flies,
> Lives in Eternity's sunrise.

Thus Buddhists (like modern physicists) don't speak of objects as things or substances, they speak of *events* that are now here (time) and now gone (movement). Indeed, Buddhists have as their primary image the "wheel of life" or *mandala*, which symbolizes continual birth, death, and rebirth.

Buddhist practitioners teach us to avoid painful human attachments by visualizing how our loved one might look in a coffin, dismembered, as a skeleton, or in an advanced stage of decomposition. Feeling a little queasy right now? That's what it's like to meditate deeply on impermanence. So odd is this visualization that Westerners don't merely shun it, they often take a certain sense of pride in the lengths they're willing to go to repress all notions of death until the very last minute. We use euphemisms and circumlocutions to dance around the word *death*. We say that a person has passed on, has met his demise, has been carried off by Jesus (or by angels), has expired, has crossed the bar (we can thank Tennyson for that one), or has kicked the bucket. The Italians have a truly wonderful expression to indicate that an individual has died and has been interred in one of their many cemeteries dominated by Italian cypress: they say that the person has gone to *gli alberi pizzuti*—to the pointy trees.

We in the West actually go so far as to paint (the only word that seems appropriate) our corpses so that they look like they're going out on the town instead of into the ground. We gather around and remark, "How lifelike she looks." This pleases the mortician, offers some sad comfort to the family, and carries us further away from the notion that someone we love has just died.

Early Griefwork Models: Freud, Bowlby, and Parkes

Sigmund Freud, along with John Bowlby and Colin Murray Parkes, founded the "griefwork" models of psychotherapy, although the trio paid scant attention to how grief and healing depend greatly on a griever's individual circumstances. In *Mourning and Melancholia* (1917), *Herr Doktor* was perhaps more realistic than the Buddha when he wrote that life consists of building attachments (relationships) and then letting go of them, a difficult and time-consuming task. Time doesn't heal everything, said Freud, you must work at it. And if Freud figured out how to live life without making attachments, as the Buddha taught, he didn't get around to writing about it.

John Bowlby, roughly contemporaneous to Freud, saw that grief has an outstanding influence on human behavior, especially on children, whose job it is to detach from their mothers. He saw that attachment could be thought of as a natural bond that stems from our biological need for security. When this bond is severed, extreme stress (separation anxiety) occurs, whether the griever is an infant, an adolescent, or an adult. Only through time can the griever "work through" or accept the loss and become freed from the attachment. The grief model that Bowlby developed consists of four phases:

- Numbing that usually lasts from a few hours to a week and may be interrupted by outbursts of extremely intense distress and/or anger
- Yearning and searching for the lost figure that lasts months or years
- Disorganization and despair
- A greater or lesser degree of organization

Colin Murray Parkes believed that it isn't just separation anxiety that creates bereavement, it is a multitude of factors. Parkes listed many of what he termed "antecedent factors" (childhood experiences, depression, kinship, gender, personality, religion, strength of the attachment, and ambivalence in a relationship) and identified three central components to bereavement:

- Preoccupation with thoughts of the deceased
- Repeatedly going over the loss experience in one's mind to test its reality
- Attempts to explain the loss or make some sense of the death

Task Models of Grief: Lindemann, Worden, and Rando

"Task models" of grieving, put forth by therapists such as Erich Lindemann, William Worden, and Therese Rando, followed the griefwork models.

Lindemann's *Symptomology and Management of Acute Grief* (1944) described his interviews with 101 recently bereaved people who had lost a loved one in 1942's Cocoanut Grove nightclub fire in Boston. Almost 500 died in this fire, many of them young Boston College boosters there to celebrate what should have been a football victory over archrival Holy Cross. Similar responses that Lindemann noted among those he interviewed included:

- Somatic or bodily distress
- Preoccupation with the deceased's image
- Guilt relating to the deceased or to the circumstances of the death
- Hostile reactions
- Adopting mannerisms and traits of the deceased
- Inability to function as competently as prior to the loss

Lindemann found that in order to establish some sort of "equilibrium," the mourners:

- Accepted the loss as a definite fact
- Adjusted to life without the deceased
- Formed new relationships

William Worden, in *Grief Counseling and Grief Therapy* (1982), wrote that rather than a vague "letting go" of grief, those who mourn must complete a set of tasks, his "Four Tasks of Mourning":

- Accept the reality of the loss
- Work through the pain of grief
- Adjust to a changed environment
- Emotionally relocate the deceased, and move on with life

Worden believed that rather than being passive about losses, the bereaved need to be active and self-determining. Like Therese Rando (but unlike Freud), he saw that the deceased could remain in the life of a person as an important relationship, albeit a much-changed and much different relationship.

A third task model therapist, Therese Rando, author of *Grief, Dying and Death* (1984), allowed the deceased to play a large role in the life of the mourner, but reframed the role not as a relationship but as a "cherished memory." Rando's stages of grief are known as the "Six R's":

- Recognize the loss, acknowledge the death, and understand its ramifications
- React to the separation of the loss; experience the pain and its myriad of emotions
- Recollect and re-experience the deceased and the relationship that was severed
- Relinquish attachments to the deceased
- Readjust to move adaptively into the "new world" without forgetting the deceased
- Re-invest the "freed up" energy into a new life or identity

The Process Model of Grief: Kübler-Ross

It wasn't until the late 1960s, in the work of Swiss clinician-researcher Elisabeth Kübler-Ross, that grief was identified as a *process*—a progressive, forward movement from one point to another on the way toward a contemplated end. In her seminal work, *On Death and Dying,* the noted thanatologist said that grief was a somewhat well-defined path that eventually led to acceptance of loss. Kübler-

Ross wrote that most of the patients she researched displayed five stages in the grieving process:

- Stage 1: Denial and isolation *("This can't be happening.")*
- Stage 2: Anger *("Why me?")*
- Stage 3: Bargaining *("What if I...?")*
- Stage 4: Depression *("I guess this is happening.")*
- Stage 5: Acceptance *("It's beginning to be okay.")*

She was quick to note that no one travels this path in exactly the same way. Still, more or less, this is the path. Her critics, and there are many, claim that in her stages, the *description* has become the *prescription*. That while she may have been correct in observing how her patients coped with death, an error may lie in her insistence that this is the way all of us *should* progress in our grief.

By numbering her grief stages, by establishing a flowchart toward ultimate closure, by making "acceptance" the home plate of the stages, and by becoming so widely read and popular, Kübler-Ross may have unwittingly allowed her opponents to crucify her on the altar of expediency. The five Kübler-Ross grief stages have become so accepted that family members and support groups may attempt to force a bereaved individual to "step lively" toward the next stage before he or she is ready; they may express impatience and actually shame a griever for reluctance to move toward acceptance. Nevertheless, Kübler-Ross is seen as the mother of the modern hospice movement, and most psychotherapists value her work.

It is instructive to note that Kübler-Ross's students (and therapists) began using an acronym, DABDA, to help remember the five grief stages. This tool has been so successful that one important feature of her first stage has been virtually forgotten. Ask anyone familiar with Kübler-Ross's work, and they will answer that "denial" is her first stage, forgetting that throughout her life, she insisted that the first stage is denial and *isolation*. Anyone who has worked with grieving people, whether they are in a psychotherapeutic relationship or in a substance abuse clinic, are well aware that when the shock of death or loss occurs, isolation and loneliness come hard on its heels.

Isolation often occurs because we don't yet have a language to describe our loss. We shun our family and friends because what has happened is either shaming to us or so far outside the bounds of normal life that we are caught unprepared. This well-documented observation—that isolation follows the shock of grief—may stem from a primitive instinct for survival. No therapist should find retreat into isolation unusual unless it continues to the point of psychopathology. However, psychotherapists should take pains to *remember* isolation; if isolation remains out of mind, the therapist will lose a great opportunity to challenge and normalize the patient.

Application of Grief Stages to Non-Death Grieving

Social gerontologist Robert Atchley, in "A Continuity Theory of Normal Aging," built on Kübler-Ross's foundation when he defined four states of retirement:

- The retirement event itself; an emotional, affirming, bittersweet ceremony, in which much attention is paid to past relationships and best wishes for the future. This can be seen as a time when one major *bardo* state is collapsed and another haltingly begins.
- The honeymoon period, in which the newly retired person, with his best foot forward, enters the new *bardo* state of *possibility* with élan, optimism, and, no doubt, some awkwardness.
- The depression, disengagement, and despair period, in which the newly retired person has difficulty allowing the new *bardo of possibility* to expand. This period is all the more painful if the retiree has always defined himself by his job.
- The self-construction/meaning stage, in which the retiree comes to shake off his old self-image as part of a corporation or workforce and forges a new one that puts meaning in his life. In this stage, retirement is seen not as an end but as a beginning.

Atchley does not use the term "grief" in this model, but it's clear that he's portraying stress, loss, hope, and struggle as a retiring person copes with the loss of one world and the difficulties in creating a new one.

Oliver Ross, an attorney who also holds a doctorate in behavioral health, enlists the Kübler-Ross model in his mediation practice for grief that is not associated with physical death. In *Situational Mediation: Sensible Conflict Resolution*, he wrote:

> Situational mediators recognize that most interpersonal disputes entail the loss or potential loss of relationships and that many participants are in one stage or another of a grief process with varying degrees of anger, sadness, and other emotions. Contrary to many mediators, who as a result of their training (or personal discomfort) disregard, avoid or eschew any display of emotion, situa-

tional mediators view emotional outbursts as fertile ground in which to further the mediation process.

Ross writes that whether his mediation clients are divorcing, healing family rifts, splitting up business partnerships, or disputing real estate transactions, they are facing the loss of relationships and/or material wealth—and grief soon follows. "During consultations I make it a point to introduce this [grief] process to potential participants," he writes. "I want to make it clear from the beginning that painful and confusing emotions are normal during divorce and that part of my job as mediator is to help them transition through these feelings." When his clients ask when these changes will stop, Ross reminds them that there are no absolute beginnings and endings, and that each person experiences grief differently. While one person may spend a great deal of time and energy in depression, another may move quickly to acceptance. In addition, grief stages can overlap and recur. Ross has found that attending to the grief of his clients by use of the Kübler-Ross model has allowed him to move his clients further toward mediation success and closure.

Most therapists and practitioners, however, continue to identify grief as belonging solely to physical death, and thus they miss opportunities to take their patients through non-death types of grief. In the West, *grief* is so associated with death that perhaps we should coin a new term for it. I nominate *bardo of promise* or *bardo of hope*.

3

Using Grief Stages in Individual Psychotherapy

○ ○
And the time of death is every moment.

—T. S. Eliot, *Four Quartets*

As psychotherapists, we think we know grief. When a patient presents and mentions a death in the family, we write in the patient's chart that he or she has significant grief issues. Prior to graduation or termination of the therapeutic relationship, we ask the patient to write a letter to the deceased, or we tie a message to a helium-filled balloon and launch it toward Heaven. This makes us feel good as therapists, and we are flattered when the patient verbalizes positive feelings about it. So we, and they, walk away from psychotherapy with the illusion that we've made things better. What we don't know—or perhaps don't want to know—is that we have entirely missed the vast majority of the patient's issues of *between*. Not only that, we've ignored, failed to recognize, or have been blinded to the most significant issue a patient has—acceptance of The Truth of Impermanence.

Recognizing Patients' *Between* States

Let's meet "Barbara," a composite psychotherapy patient. Barbara presents for counseling, fills out her admission papers, and enters the counseling office. Nervous, she sits with her purse in her lap until gently told by her therapist that it's okay to place the purse in a more comfortable position. Realizing that clutching her purse is silly and has betrayed her nervousness, she sets it aside and begins to engage with the therapist in what is termed a "therapeutic relationship."

Barbara tells the therapist that her mood has been rather low of late. (She may be past the denial stage about her mood to the extent that she actually uses the word *depression,* but chances are she'll rely on euphemisms such as *down, low,* or *flat.*) She's aging, she says, her kids are transitioning to high school and work, old friends are moving to faraway cities, her father is in assisted living, her husband has announced that he will soon take a three-week business trip, her purse was just stolen, and she's concerned that she may lose her job due to corporate restructuring. Barbara then mentions that her mother died last summer and that she hasn't been quite the same since.

Most often, the therapist will listen to all this and conclude that Barbara is stressed and depressed because of her mother's death, and depending on the severity of her depression, medication may be prescribed. All the other forms of grief that Barbara is experiencing, all the *bardo* states, are ignored—perhaps because of the therapist's inability to deal with The Truth of Impermanence in his own life (see Chapter 1). Therapists who have studied their own grief will more quickly identify the grief cycles and states of *between* in their clients.

Not all the blame falls to the therapist. The *Diagnostic & Statistical Manual IV* (the so-called Bible of psychotherapy, also known as DSM-IV) fails to mention the word *grief*—and if the DSM doesn't mention grief, managed care won't pay for grief therapy. DSM-IV does, however, go to great lengths to constellate the symptoms of depression and anger, though it doesn't see them in terms of grief, and it certainly doesn't see grief as a subset of a *bardo* state. Likewise, in most psychotherapy texts and self-help books, the word *guilt* appears often, but *grief* is rarely mentioned. Look up *time* in any mental health or behavioral health text and you'll come away empty handed.

To be fair, DSM-IV does mention *bereavement* (V62.82). It points out that grieving patients may present with symptoms that mimic a major depressive episode, although that diagnosis should be deferred until two months following the loss. That is to say, a certain amount of time must pass before a diagnosis of *major* depression is teased from *situational* depression. DSM-IV further points out that cultural norms vary extensively, so the therapist should strive to understand the cultural context of a patient before making a more serious bereavement diagnosis. However, if a patient mentions that she in some way inadvertently contributed to the death, if she assumes what is known as "survivor guilt," if she comes to believe that she should have died with the deceased, if she begins to see or hear the deceased person, the therapist will catch on that normal grief has somehow morphed into pathological grief.

Most often, psychotherapists depend on a patient to self-disclose grief. During a clinical assessment, therapists don't ask about children taken from the home by Child Protective Services, miscarriages, stillbirths, abortions, and loss of childhood due to dysfunctional parents. Patients are never asked whether reproductive difficulties have resulted in the absence of children and grandchildren (the grief of something that never happened). But these lie in the patient's mind like scars on the body; they're constant reminders of something that happened (or failed to happen) long ago.

Failure to help bring a client to an understanding of life's impermanence is unethical, and it can't be gotten around merely by saying, "If I disabuse her of the notion that life features anything of permanence, she'll become depressed and regress in treatment." This is tantamount to buying into the patient's illusion of permanence. The therapist may wish to suggest that a patient live his life within a religious or spiritual framework. But it's wrong to hinder a patient who is prepared to come to grips with The Truth of Impermanence simply because the therapist cannot handle it. The idea of psychotherapy is to empower the patient to shun illusions—and the illusion of permanence is about as big an illusion as we can have.

It is not necessary that the patient, especially during acute grief, be told about impermanence. It's not necessary to scare a patient about grief or to even mention the impermanence of life. However, patients can be prepared for the grief that inevitably follows loss and separation. "Don't drown patients in truth; only God can take away hope," was the way Kübler-Ross put it. In fact, most *bardo* states do not require treatment. *Bardo* states (or a multiplicity of *between* states) are not disease. Acute *bardo* states, such as death, trauma, and other major transitions can and should be treated; however, chronic *bardo* states (such as aging and major life transitions) can be addressed simply by the Buddhist concept of "mindfulness." Those who choose to live life to the fullest should be aware of the *bardo* states and accept them as a major fact of life.

It may be helpful for the patient to maintain a workbook detailing the various *between* states she's going through (see Chapter 1). This can be considered "journaling." You don't need to be obsessive or compulsive about this. The idea is to understand that you have a few acute *bardo* states and many chronic *bardo* states underway at every given moment.

Patients like Barbara don't need to become "diagnosis victims" or overwhelmed by the sheer number of *between* states. However, the therapist who attempts to understand The Truth of Impermanence can gently normalize Barbara's *between* states and help her see the key role they play in her life. And certainly, grief can be seen as a positive experience, as a valuable opportunity for making major life and personality changes. It can be reframed, in other words, from a negative to a positive experience.

In fact, grief is very often associated with joy. The graduation of a son or daughter who has been accepted into college is an occasion for great celebration, along with heart-rending moments in which the parent thinks, "My baby's all grown up." The marriage of an adult child is another occasion that leads to both joy and sorrow. It's a major rite of passage, but it shatters the parents' illusion that the child will always remain small and dependent. Likewise, the death of a parent after a long, painful illness is often tinged by both sadness and relief: "It's a blessing" is what we'll often hear when we express our sorrow to their adult children. Some patients repress their sense of relief following the death of a suffering parent thinking that it's unseemly to feel that way. A therapist can normalize this and show the patient how grief often peacefully coexists with relief.

It's important that patients in psychotherapy understand the role of grief before leaving treatment. In fact, it's beneficial to explore the grief associated with graduating or leaving treatment. Therapists who have worked in substance abuse treatment may smile as they recall patients who gleefully counted down the number of days until "graduation"—until about three days prior to the occasion, whereupon the patient suddenly turned sullen and fearful. The fear is there because the treatment center has served as a safe haven, and the patient is scared to leave. An observant clinician will deal with this fear by anticipating it, talking about it during group process, and gradually "stepping down" the patient into less-intensive therapeutic settings such as outpatient treatment, aftercare groups, and support groups.

Anger As a Grief Stage

Anger management has become such a staple of modern-day psychotherapy that it has come to be spoofed by Hollywood. Those with anger problems, whether they are involved in domestic violence, road rage, or workplace incidents, are routinely placed into process groups in which they are taught such behavior modification skills as identifying a potential problem, deescalating the anger, and practicing new coping skills that reframe a negative into a positive.

Anger is a feeling—one of the classic ones. Anger is normal and useful; so useful, in fact, that it was and is important to our survival as a species. Without anger, humankind may not have developed the "fight or flight" capabilities that led us out of Africa as a strange new animal capable of abstract thought and unparalleled manual dexterity.

Anger, and the clear, direct expression it produces, can result in meaningful communication. But anger is most often used to mask fear. We may not be comfortable with other feelings, but when we place them under the aegis of anger, we're in our comfort zone. As long as we look angry, we think, no one will suspect that we're terrified. When we implode all our emotions into one single emotion—anger—our coping skills become extremely limited, and we're likely to find ourselves in anger management classes.

Anger comes in many flavors. We can choose from a menu that includes anger avoidance, sneaky anger, distrustful/paranoid anger, sudden anger, shame-based anger, deliberate anger, adrenaline anger, habitual anger, moral anger, and grudge anger. But whatever kind of anger it is, we can learn to control it and get our needs met another way.

It's important to remember that anger is different from rage. Rage is not a feeling, it is a manipulative tool that ensures we get exactly what we want; it is used for control and for accumulation of power. Anger is often subconscious, but rage is always conscious. Ragers learn to turn their fury off and on as the situation requires. Rage is rewarded, and as with other behaviors that are rewarded, it is often repeated. Those who rage most often learn this maladaptive coping skill in childhood and never grow out of it—until they run afoul of the law.

Anger is a major grief stage into which we lapse as soon as denial and isolation yield the field: Why did this happen to me? Why do things need to change so much? Why do people need to die? Why does life need to be so impermanent? How do I deal with all the changes that are happening to me at every given moment?

Anger is often the result of unmet expectations. I walk out of the house in the morning, back my car out of the driveway, and mentally run through all the things that I'm going to get done today. Then reality intervenes. Very soon, I realize that my day is hopelessly out of control and all my careful plans must be abandoned. I get angry and don't know what to do with it. In other words, I made the mistake of planning my day and got angry because life had other ideas. I'm grieving the loss of my carefully planned day.

As we've seen, delving into The Truth of Impermanence is the not for the faint of heart. We have adapted, we have evolved a high degree of consciousness, we live our lives and are able to procreate because of impermanence. But when we're faced with it, it's certainly not what we expected. We need a sense of permanence, and all we get are thousands of change states. "It's not what I expected;

it's not what I want; I don't feel comfortable with all this change, and I want it to stop." Considering all the *bardo* states we're in, no wonder we're angry.

Anger is often, but not always, very visible (especially when a coworker punches a hole in a wall or brings a gun to work), but we don't always see the grief behind it. That's a major failing of Western psychiatry: *We treat anger as a stand-alone diagnosis.* Were we to see it *always* as a grief stage, we would automatically look for the disappointment, the loss, the pain, and the unmet expectations behind it. This can be as simple as saying that my carefully planned day fell apart—or as tough as unresolved family-of-origin issues.

When we first met composite patient Barbara, she sounded depressed because of all the changes that were going on around her. But let's say that rather than feeling "blue," she is angry. She tells her therapist that her husband has suddenly been called upon to take a long business trip, her child is off to college, her mother had just died, and her friends are gradually moving away. The therapist, seeing that Barbara can barely contain herself, might merely note that the patient had severe anger issues and suggest anger management, relaxation tapes, or chamomile tea. However, if the therapist were more observant, he might ask Barbara about her life history and perhaps see how all her states of change, all her *bardo* states, were conspiring against her. Desperately seeking permanence, all she got was a truckload of impermanence, and in the midst of this, anger showed up like an unwanted relative.

The angry Barbara needs a therapist who understands that all anger is a grief stage, and that grief is always the most visible of all *bardo* states. Barbara would benefit from a rational-emotive challenge to her underlying belief that life should be static and unchanging. Barbara could come to see that impermanence rules our lives and that she is stuck in the anger stage of grief. Getting her unstuck depends on how skilled the therapist is in understanding The Truth of Impermanence and its powerful effect on all of us.

Depression As a Grief Stage

Generalized sadness, lack of interest in things that are normally pleasurable, difficulty eating and sleeping—these are symptoms of classic depression. When they result from advanced substance abuse or the death of a loved one, they may be temporary in nature and slowly subside upon addiction recovery or acceptance of the death. This we term "acute depression," and after a short regimen of talk therapy and antidepressants, the symptoms are generally extinguished.

If, however, there's a family history of depression, if the onset of depression occurs during adolescence and continues well into adulthood, if the depression cannot be associated with a single traumatic event, this may not be acute depression but *chronic* depression. This calls for a more aggressive approach by the psychotherapist, as well as acceptance by the depressed patient that, unlike a common cold, the depression will not spontaneously disappear. The patient must show more diligence in keeping this chronic depression at bay, and he must place this disability at or near the top of his list of priorities.

Initiating factors for acute and chronic depression will be looked for, but rare is the therapist who knows that depression *must always be seen as a stage of grief.* Most often, the therapist will simply make note of the fact that the patient has a long history of depression, that there's probably difficulty in transferring messages from his presynaptic neurons through the synapse to his postsynaptic neurons, but will miss the fact that the patient has suffered a loss and is actually locked in a grief stage called depression. The grief is symptomatic of either a short or incredibly long *bardo* state.

Perhaps the patient's *bardo* or change state is due to his or her perception that life is incredibly difficult and that he feels powerless to call a halt to it. Perhaps, like Barbara, the patient lacks the ego strength to collapse a painful *bardo* state and move into another that's tolerable, if not pleasurable. If the attending therapist is not well versed in The Truth of Impermanence, most likely he will simply be glad to help the patient become free of acute depression but will fail to grasp that the patient is dealing with dozens of *bardo* states that come her way. If the therapist were to explain to the patient how many change states were occurring at any given moment and empower her to understand how much flux these change states bring into her life, perhaps the patient could see that life is made up of change, that there's no escaping it, and that it can't be dealt with by getting and staying depressed. This is not to say that antidepressants or other psychopharmaceuticals don't need to be involved initially, but clearly, treating depression (like anger) outside of the larger context of grief can be thought of as a failure of modern psychotherapy. Just as much a failure as not seeing grief as a subset of minor and major *bardo* states.

Who Is Allowed to Grieve and Who Isn't

Psychotherapists understand that in our society, we place strict rules on who can grieve and who can't. For example, we allow victims to grieve, but we cringe when a perpetrator grieves. Do the German and Japanese nations have a right to grieve the hardships they experienced during World War II? Or is grieving the sole right of the victors? A firestorm of public indignation followed a *Milwaukee Journal-Sentinel* story about an elderly Milwaukee woman of German heritage who had written a self-published book about the hardships she and her family suffered in Germany from the mid-1930s to 1945. A huge number of letters to the editor blasted this woman for daring to grieve her girlhood under the Third Reich.

Not only do we try to control who can grieve and who can't, we often allow our value systems to limit grief to those whom we feel are truly worthy. For instance, if a patient presents for treatment with grief due to the loss of a child or a life partner, we understand this grief, attend it, use active listening skills, summarize, and provide unconditional positive regard. This is true grief, we tell ourselves, and it brings our compassion to the fore.

But what if a well-dressed man presents for treatment because a hurricane recently destroyed one of his yachts? We learn that although he has several expensive watercraft, this one had been, by far, his favorite. In fact, it had been a gift from his tycoon father when he turned 21. The patient is obviously distraught, and he cries tears that are just as hot and heavy as a person who has lost a child. As therapists, do we catch ourselves judging this person? In a small part of our brain, do we hear a judgmental voice that wants to ask, "You're seeing a therapist because you lost a *boat?*" Well, as a matter of fact, he is. In scenarios like this, our prejudices may tempt us to pay less attention to a griever because we consider his loss unworthy of our attention, or we resent that he's taking valuable therapeutic time away from other more deserving patients. But this griever is in emotional pain, and it's not up to us to discount it because his values appear to differ from our own. We are professionally obligated to be with each patient wherever he or she is at the moment and to resist being judgmental.

Interactions with Those in Other Grief Stages

It's important, too, to keep in mind that few people go through the grief stages in the same way or at the same rate. In early 2003, my wife interrupted a home burglary and was knocked semiconscious by two adolescents in the foyer of our home. Because we had been involved in the addiction recovery movement for two decades and were familiar with the grief stages, we went through them rather quickly and soon entered the acceptance stage. However, when we found ourselves speaking with close friends and family members who seemed stuck in the anger and depression stages, we were perplexed. Only when we figured out that few of our friends and family members had any experience with grief stages did this start making sense to us.

Those who continued to express anger, we realized, were subconsciously telling us that they loved us and wanted to protect us. Others equated our eventual acceptance of the attack with dropping the incident from our minds. When one friend was told that words of forgiveness were included in our remarks to the judge at the sentencing hearing for one of the perpetrators, he bristled, "Well, why don't you just adopt him?" We saw then that others were grieving at a different pace. We ultimately learned to ask each family member and friend to try his or her best to understand where we were, and to strive to support us in the difficult decision-making process we were facing.

Another example of how those in various grief stages interact every single day can be found in an examination of the process of a person being terminated from a job. Let's say that you are a manager, and you've slowly come to the conclusion that employee "Bob" must be laid off as your company downsizes. A few weeks ago, when this necessity became apparent, there was some hesitation on your part as you entered the *denial* stage of grief. As you came out of denial, you slowly entered the *anger* phase: "Why does this have to happen to a great worker like Bob?" you asked yourself. Shifting to *bargaining*, you began to conjure up all sorts of scenarios of how Bob could survive the layoff. None of these scenarios really made sense, and you entered the *depression* phase, in which you slipped into restless nights and loss of appetite. As you left that phase, you entered into full *acceptance*—an understanding that there's no longer room for Bob in your workforce, and he's better off getting on with his life as he exits your company and enters another one. You've had plenty of time to progress through the grief stages, and for the first time in weeks, you're calm and collected as you arrange a meeting to give Bob the bad news. Bob arrives at the meeting, and you make it clear that—nothing personal—his employment has been terminated. Stunned at what he's hearing, Bob enters the denial-isolation phase of the grief process. A glance from another cubicle at this knee-to-knee encounter between you and Bob will seem ordinary. But in fact, it typifies many of the daily encounters that take place between people in different stages of the grief process.

Understanding "Control Freaks" in Terms of *Bardo* States

"Control freak" is a popular term used to refer to those who absolutely believe that they must be in control of everything in their lives at all times. A more self-defeating illusion cannot be found. It's usually the residue of an old coping skill left over from family-of-origin issues. Perhaps it worked during childhood and adolescence, but fails in the complexities of adulthood.

In my view, "control freaks" are unschooled in The Truth of Impermanence. They live in the illusion of control to ensure their lives are not upset by options and changes—a truly irrational notion. They are afraid of *between* states and spend much time and personal energy ensuring that they ignore reality.

Some years back, a popular television program called *Dharma & Greg* illustrated how far some people will go to try to prevent change, yet how far others will venture in the boundary-less embrace of any and all *bardo* states. The premise of this show was that the Montgomerys (Kitty and Edward) are rock-ribbed Republicans, industrial tycoons, givers of charity balls, and, basically, repressed Puritans. Their uptight son Greg, in a moment of distraction, has married Dharma, a sprightly young woman who is the illegitimate daughter of two free-spirited socialists named Abby and Larry. Lifelong hippies, Abby and Larry have never abandoned the counterculture lifestyle—they drive a VW microbus and regard the consumption of dairy and meat products as the root of all health problems. These sitcom families sort out a litany of misunderstandings every week, and viewers are hard pressed to determine which family is stranger.

There is not much exploration of how the two families repress the notion of impermanence, but it is clear that the Montgomerys are terrified of change and will do everything in their power to collapse any *bardo* state that comes along. Edward Montgomery's drug of choice in this vain attempt is expensive, single-malt Scotch, and he indulges in it whenever he can. Kitty medicates her long-repressed feelings with a combination of control and money. Larry and Abby, in direct contrast to their counterparts, the Montgomerys, are so open to any type of change that they drive themselves crazy embracing each of the exponentially increasing *bardo* states that open before them. Larry copes with his unbounaried life by growing and smoking marijuana to the point of paranoia. In each episode, Dharma and Greg fight to maintain some sort of balance as their families rocket off to wherever their Brooks Brothers clothing or tie-dyed dashikis take them. They try, as a couple, to compromise between rigidity and chaos—the recipe for a calm, abiding life.

Self-Esteem and *Bardo* States

Nathaniel Branden, a popular psychotherapist, author, and trainer who researched and practiced the psychology of self-esteem long before it became a household word, has an interesting take on how a change state, or a state of *between*, affects the way a person feels about himself. Branden writes that a major change in occupation can actually turn a person who seems full of self-esteem into a mass of self-doubt. He asks us to envision an individual who works in, say, the information services (IS) department of a major corporation. This person is in her "comfort zone" and is happy. She looks forward to coming to work each day and does such a good job that laudatory employee evaluations and salary increases are common occurrences. She is viewed by coworkers as happy, adjusted, and self-reliant, and from the water cooler to the office lunch room, she is often the subject of envy.

Then one day, this happy, self-confident person gets a promotion. From the IS department she is sent to the marketing department where she is asked to meet and greet product consumers and buyers. Almost overnight, colleagues see a different person emerge. Gone is the confident worker, and in its place is a nervous, awkward person who is full of anxiety. So ill-at-ease is this person that her coworkers soon realize that her self-esteem wasn't really what Branden calls self-esteem at all. It was merely the manifestation of a person in her personal zone of comfort. Change that comfort zone, place that person into a state of *between*, and you find a person drowning in fear. This person was "busted," to use today's vernacular. What appeared to be self-esteem in a zone of comfort suddenly appeared to be a mass of self-doubt in another, less familiar job.

Branden's solution would be for the employee to practice his six steps to self-esteem so that she could gain true self-worth, regardless of the job she occupies. Self-esteem, says Branden, is much more than the simple recitation of daily affirmations or standing in front of a mirror and saying, "You look great, Handsome!" Branden writes that true self-esteem has two constituent parts: *self-efficacy*, a sense of basic confidence in the face of life's challenges, and *self-respect*, a sense of being worthy of happiness. Taken together, self-esteem can be thought of as an immune system, providing resistance, strength, and an ability to deal with life's many states of *between*.

Viewing Neurosis and Psychosis in Terms of *Bardo* States

Another way in which we may see *bardo* states as alternately comforting and anxiety-producing is in the different approaches to the treatment of neurosis and psychosis. Neurotic patients may be thought of as bound up; essentially, in a mental straightjacket. They are in touch with reality but are often paralyzed with fear, marginalized by anger, and catatonic with repressed feelings. Analysts and therapists have long known that such emotionally bound-up people must learn to open up, to talk, to share, to laugh, to write, to hug, to cry, and to ask assertively for what they need. They may begin this process with a therapist and continue it with trusted family and friends. They may attend a solid support group and use that group to share the secrets that are keeping them sick. But no doubt about it, to treat neurosis is to teach the many ways of self-expression that lead to relatively pain-free living.

Psychosis, losing touch with reality, is different from neurosis, and it calls for entirely different treatment. Psychosis is a borderless world in which voices are heard and thoughts are generated that are quite out of the realm of experience for more than 99% of the general population. A good visualization of what psychosis may look like can be found in the 2001 film, *A Beautiful Mind*, which tells the story of John F. Nash, whose work in game theory led to a Nobel Prize in Economic Sciences. Psychosis is an isolating fragmentation of the personality that almost always results in severe dysfunction for sufferers, their families, and their job systems.

A psychotherapist treating an individual with psychosis would not want to "open him up" in the way he would a neurotic; the psychotic needs to be contained. In my practice, I've met only a few who presented for treatment in active psychosis, and I quickly stopped the treatment procedure, allowed the patient to relax in the waiting room, and sought referral to a much higher level of care. A decision to "open up" a person who was experiencing auditory or visual hallucinations would be harmful and extremely unethical.

My practice has always been limited to substance abuse treatment, and if there's any better way to hop the train headed for neurosis, this is it. Mood-altering chemicals, at first, seem to expand the number of available change states. Life seems unlimited, and an illusion of well-being sets in. After awhile, the substance-abusing person, as drug tolerance increases, begins to see fewer and fewer opportunities; later, she sees no way out, begins to isolate, and her neurosis deepens to the point of stupefaction.

Another way of looking at this is through the world of *bardo* states. It may be that one becomes neurotic by events and triggers that shut down a patient's world view to the degree that the patient perceives no states of change available to her. The worse the neurosis, the fewer the change states that seem attainable. The patient retreats to a darkened room, and suicidal ideation is not far off. Treatment, then, comes in the form of working with the neurotic patient to allow her to both talk and write until she sees the many available states of *between*.

Those with psychosis, on the other hand, may be thought of as having an illness wherein their *bardo* states are unlimited and exploding at an exponential rate. Seeking to cope with this, they engage with their voices or personalities in the vain attempt to mediate with them. Thus treatment of the psychotic can be thought of as collapsing or severely limiting their states of change to levels that produce calmness and stability.

Guiding Patients from Content to Process

Another way of seeing how *bardo* states affect us is to watch a good therapist calm a patient who is deep into *content* by transforming her over time into a person of *process*. The term *content* is used here to denote the minutia of daily life. Content is the many scattered fragments of life that, without organization, make little sense. Content is what your teenager talks about for hours on the phone; it's the small talk at the hair salon and the conversation around the television during the playoffs—the descriptive recalling of who did what, and when. Content is trivia that has yet to be elevated to meaning.

And *meaning* is a good word to describe process. Process is what is left over when you stop describing what you did and start wondering what led you to do it. Process is the vowels and content is the consonants. To use another analogy, bread cannot be made with flour alone. Water (or some other liquid) is needed to hold the whole thing together. Flour can be seen as *content* and water as the *process* that gives shape and meaning to the flour.

In psychotherapy, many new patients are so deep into content, into minutia and trivia, that they are riddled with anxiety. The head of the therapist nearly spins as the patient pours out a stream of disjointed content. No item is too minor for the patient; in fact, all content seemingly takes on the same weight. A broken transmission is given exactly the same emotional heft as a sudden demand for divorce. A broken fingernail is at parity with the sudden death of a parent. If the therapist were to ask, "What do you make of all this?" most likely the patient would have no idea. And perhaps that's why he is in treatment. He lives his life in minutia and has no idea how to process it—how to make it all make sense.

It's no surprise that such patients live in anxiety. In their world, where major concerns such as safety, family, financial security, and physical health rank no higher than trivial concerns such as who was in what movie and where to get a certain brand of kitty litter, anxiety will prevail as the world becomes stranger and stranger. In our *bardo* state model, we can say that this patient who lives and works in content is anxious because they see too many *bardo* states opening up around them and cannot judge which are more important than others. Only when a therapist teaches the patient to get out of content and into process can the patient see how it's all connected. And only when the therapist empowers the patient to collapse exploding *bardo* states can the patient begin to feel the calmness that such activities bring.

This is not easy, nor does it come all at once. But a therapist brave enough to swim upstream into a fast-moving river of content will hear from time to time a classic "feeling word" (e.g., *mad, sad, glad, hurt, ashamed,* or *afraid*), and when she hears it, she will begin to dismantle the content machine gun and strive ever so slowly to win the patient over toward organizing his life and becoming aware of what's keeping him stuck. In other words, the therapist helps collapse the many *bardo* states that are drowning the patient by teaching him to focus on the various functional and dysfunctional ways he deals with life.

Frankl's "Sunday Neurosis" As a *Bardo* State

To understand *bardo* states, one need look no further than childhood feelings about Sundays. This was a day on which each schoolchild stood on the cusp, in a gap, on a bridge between school and the freedom a weekend promised. Saturdays were fun—friends were met and bikes were ridden. Homework assignments were postponed, and the shackles of academia were shaken off. Then came Sunday. For many, the "Sunday problem" didn't rear its ugly head until after Sunday morning church services. That's when the "Sunday feeling" set in. Homework loomed, freedom would cease in a few hours, meals became more and more unstructured, and a kind of malaise set in.

Adults notice this too. Sunday means that the weekend is winding down and the rat race will begin in a few short hours. "Why can't we have three-day weekends?" we always ask. Fueled by caffeine, we shake off the state of relaxation that we experienced on Friday and Saturday and enter the state of Monday morning tension that results when humorless supervisors, production schedules, and sales goals slap us in the face. And we certainly notice that changing such states is even tougher after vacations and long holiday breaks.

Viktor Frankl called this the "Sunday neurosis," and he blamed it on the depression that people got when they entered and exited a gap between pressure and boredom. In our *bardo* model, we can easily see that we are changing *bardo* states, and once done, we can relax again. Work goes well until Friday, when we again change *bardo* states. It's as if we don't dread work or play, pressure or boredom, so much as the state of change that exists between them.

About the Word *Closure*

It became more than apparent after the Oklahoma City bombing and the September 11 terrorist attacks that the word *closure* had a pejorative ring to it. The word had originally meant a "finalization" of the grief process, a moving on in life to where the victim of a trauma accepted and dealt with her loss. However, victims of these and other tragedies began to spurn the word and felt insulted if it was brought up during an interview. The therapeutic community soon saw that they had failed to effectively communicate why closure is so important to healing. Perhaps these grieving family members were stuck in the *anger* phase of the Kübler-Ross model, or perhaps they mistakenly equated closure with forgetting about the death. Perhaps they saw closure as an excuse to let the offending terrorist off without consequences for his heinous acts. On television, we heard them saying things like, "I'll never have closure; I'll always remember my daughter, and I can't rest until her killer is tracked down and executed."

This is certainly putting conditions on your healing, and therapists aren't at all surprised when the execution comes and goes and the survivor's emotional wounds remain. The same phenomenon occurs when an ethnic group or an individual demands restitution or an apology from a government. When a dollar figure is finally offered, they will say, "How can you put a price on the value of my great-grandfather?" Or, if an apology that was demanded is made, the victim will sniff that it's "too little, too late."

In any case, *closure* quickly became a buzzword, and we almost hesitate to use it anymore, whether in a news interview, a therapeutic relationship, or with a family friend. Whether the word will remain in current usage or will be banished to some dark cellar remains to be seen. It would indeed be sad to allow words such as *closure, acceptance,* and even *forgiveness* to be hijacked by a vocal minority and come to mean cowardice—especially in the United States, which likes to think of itself as a compassionate nation.

Bardo State Awareness in Treating Adolescents

Is there any greater, more visible, or more painful state of *between* than adolescence? Think of it. We are caught between the developmental stages of childhood and adulthood; our bodies are maturing sexually (although cognitively we remain ill-equipped for it); we are caught between dolls and mortgage payments, between Power Rangers and power bills; and as the Victorians once said, it seems as if one life is dying while the other is powerless to be born.

Outside the context of a grief state, it's easy to laugh at the awkwardness of this stage of development. But placed into the context of a *bardo* state, we can see adolescence as a state of *grief*, a state of change where the adolescent is awkward and off-balance at best, and downright suicidal at worst. Seeing adolescence as a state of grief or a major *bardo* state gives it the respect it deserves and explains why the time is so painful. Perhaps it is painful because adolescence is a developmental period where anxiety is produced because there are too many *bardos*.

One way to reduce this anxiety is to allow (and expect) teenagers to test limits. Indeed, testing limits is one of their jobs. As he separates himself from the security of childhood, the teenager is not sure how far he can go in his new transition state. It's up to the adults in his life to put up the appropriate boundaries. He may tell you he doesn't like them, but deep down, these boundaries are welcome and help collapse the *bardo* state he's in.

The other major job for teenagers is to make poor choices (working two jobs is why they're always so tired and hungry). They learn from experience, and experience comes from making poor choices. This is not fun, but making poor choices leads to consequences and the making of better choices.

Trust is a major issue with adolescents. Any adult going through a painful separation or grief issue puts a premium on trust. So, too, with adolescents. They're in murky, unfamiliar territory and they need guidance. They're willing enough to trust you, but you'd better not let them down. They are very into the "now." They are often embarrassed by the fact that not long ago, they were infants (show them a baby picture if you don't believe this), and they don't like to think about the past. And because the future is cloudy and full of nerdy things like full-time jobs and mortgage payments, they aren't crazy about the future, either.

They want and need physical intimacy, but they are afraid to show it. Just because a teenager, making his or her necessary transition from cartoons to car payments, tells you he doesn't like to be coddled or kissed doesn't mean he's uninterested in relational intimacy.

Teens feel exposed as they transition to adulthood, and they respond well to rewards and consequences. One way of limiting this exposure is to reward appropriate behaviors and inhibit inappropriate behaviors with consequences. In an odd way, they prefer this because it implodes the vast, uncharted world they find themselves in.

Teens struggle with life because they are leaving concrete, abstract thinking and are entering the "gray areas." This is threatening; akin to teetering on a diving board perched high above a small pool. Gone are the old, naïve ways of thinking, and at hand is the unfamiliar world of complex thinking and a life that doesn't always end "happily ever after."

The teenage world is one in which morals and beliefs are questioned. Out of curiosity, they begin to experiment with strange beliefs and strange ways of dressing. If they have parents who are secure in their values and beliefs, this will probably remain simple experimentation.

And as every parent knows, as soon as a teenager learns the word *hypocrisy*, they, like Diogenes, take a lamp and go in search of it. And do they ever find it! They find it whenever they encounter an adult who lies to them or merely "talks the talk" rather than "walks the walk." Teens don't want to be lied to. They are insecure in their great *bardo of* change, and lying to them is a great way to turn them off.

Essentially, you get one shot at teenagers. If the reader is a parent or a psychotherapist, you will understand that you don't get many second chances with teens. They live in a topsy-turvy world where the center is not holding anymore, and they don't have much time to wait for you to prove authentic.

Bardo State Awareness in Treating the Elderly

Those at a time in their lives when retirement (or eldercare) looms are of special interest to the *bardo*-aware psychotherapist. Their gray hair, wrinkles, and physical debilitations place seniors at the polar opposite of adolescents. Younger people don't see the great *bardo of becoming* or the ephemeral nature of life. Their chief interest is how good they look, how hip they are, and how closely they can follow the latest trends in fashion and speech. The elderly, unless they are hindered by a psychiatric disorder, know full well they are losing brain weight, bone density, and muscle mass at an alarming rate. They certainly know where this all leads, but they may be pushing it out of their consciousness to the point that they are in complete denial that death is not far off. While many therapists understand that adolescents are reluctant to enter treatment because they feel too young to have major mental or behavioral health problems, many seniors forego treatment because they believe they're too old. And part of the work a therapist may need to do with an aging person is to get past the "it's too late" syndrome. As in "It's too late for me to sober up" or "It's too late for me to reconcile with my children"; in other words, "It's too late for me to begin another *bardo of becoming*."

Unlike the teen who expresses anxiety because he's overwhelmed with too many *bardo* states, the older person may feel anxiety over the fact that there are seemingly too few of them.

An older person may also be hindered by a social stigma they picked up decades ago that says only truly crazy people need psychiatric help. When they were young, psychiatry was in its infancy. Yes, they read about people who needed analysis, but didn't the motion pictures depict these people as truly psychotic? Don't mental hospitals do shock treatments, like they did on Joan Crawford in the film *Autumn Leaves*? Thus, the admission that some form of psychiatric assistance is needed may be difficult for the elderly. And often, they ride this stigma all the way to some form of fast or slow suicide.

This goes along with their belief that all addicted people stick needles in their arms or suck wine from bottles covered by paper bags. They fail to see that over-medicating themselves with alcohol and prescription pills is merely a refusal to see that a *bardo of becoming* is not just for the young. They view asking for help as a badge of shame, and they are basically unaware that they are living their lives in many states of disappointment and regret.

The elderly patient or client experiences different *bardo* states than the adolescent. In addition to leaving behind jobs, careers, the home where they raised their families, good health, and sharp memories, seniors are most often taking a long look back at what happened to their *bardo of becoming*. They most often need encouragement from therapists that this is a grief state and that what they're grieving is the normal loss of their former selves and their previous lifestyles. In fact, the crisis of aging can be reframed as a crisis of "finding meaning."

Old people, because of physical infirmities and driving restrictions, often have fewer options. This leads to a grief state in which their universe has dramatically narrowed. Those around them who are younger often grieve the thousands of choices they must make on a daily basis. But when all those choices suddenly vanish in old age, grief often appears. Thus we grieve choices and likewise grieve the lack of them.

Part of the recovery of any aged person is for them to remind themselves on a daily basis that while the number is smaller, they continue to have choices. They may no longer zoom around in a car, but they can pick up a phone and call an adult child. They may not be able to dart over to the shopping mall at will, as they once did, but they may pop in on the lonely person in the next room. They may no longer be called upon to dry tears and apply Band-Aids to scuffed knees, but they can learn to find meaning in their life and eventual death. This is liberating and something that must not be taken away from anyone at any age.

It's worthwhile to mention that old people often complain that younger people seem to pull away from them. And this is true. The young don't like to be reminded that they, too, will eventually lose their hair, their vigor, and ultimately their lives; they see the old as walking advertisements of those facts. Middle-aged children often return from the funeral of a parent only to lament, "We're now the older ones, and we're next," as if there's some sort of cosmic on-deck circle that, bat in hand, we enter upon the death of a parent.

Before we leave the elderly, let's hear from David Snowdon. In his book, *Aging with Grace: What the Nun Study Teaches Us about Leading Longer, Healthier, and More Meaningful Lives,* Snowdon wrote of a study published in 2000 by the Mayo Clinic of Rochester, Minnesota. In this study, Mayo researchers followed up on 839 former patients who had classified themselves on standardized personality tests in the early 1960s. Clinicians were surprised to find that significantly more "optimists" were alive than those who had identified themselves as "pessimists." Although clinicians were understandably hesitant to jump to conclusions based on this survey, they can't be faulted for wondering whether it was nature, nurture, or some sort of immune system benefit that did the trick. I wonder whether those with longer lives—the optimists—weren't better able to explore, deal with, and cope with the many *bardo* states that opened and closed on them every minute. Perhaps they had an ability to see positive *bardo* states opening, to close negative *bardo* states, and to understand The Truth of Impermanence.

4

Using Grief Stages in Group Psychotherapy

How old would you be if you didn't know how old you were?

—Satchel Paige

The stages or tasks of grief have many useful applications in substance abuse treatment, both in one-on-one encounters and with patients in group therapy. Whether employing grief stage models or grief task models, addiction can easily be viewed as synonymous with grief.

For the last seven years, I have volunteered at the Franciscan Renewal Center (FRC) in Paradise Valley, Arizona. This bucolic, pastoral retreat center features a sophisticated, well-managed counseling/ministry office and dozens of psychotherapists who volunteer their time either for "one-on-ones" or for process groups. A number of issues are dealt with: addiction, grief and loss, difficult adult children, divorce and separation, lack of self-esteem, parenting gays and lesbians, and surviving incest, to name but a few. All who seek treatment are received in the true spirit of St. Francis of Assisi and are provided compassionate care whether they are nonbelievers or part of a larger religious or spiritual community.

Grief Stages in an Addiction Support Group

The group that I co-facilitate is called "The Many Faces of Chemical Dependency." The group is open to everyone, but year in and year out, I would estimate that 80% of those who attend are reeling from the addiction of another. Anywhere from one to sixteen are likely to be present at a meeting, and few who attend are aware that they are in stages of denial, anger, bargaining, depression, and acceptance.

Denial and Isolation. Meeting attendees who present in *denial* are in shock. Someone in their life has just self-disclosed, and they have no clue of what to do. Their 17-year-old son may have recently committed a drug-related misdemeanor, or perhaps he announced that he's tired of doing drugs and wants to quit. Their overachiever daughter may have suddenly received a DUI or a minor-in-possession charge. Their spouse may have just been intervened upon and is now residing in a drug or alcohol treatment center.

Certainly, most people in denial and shock don't summon up the courage to attend a drop-in group in a public place right away. They first *isolate*, just as Kübler-Ross predicted they would. Eventually, this proves unworkable, and they begin to ask around or notice in their church bulletin that the FRC has an addiction group meeting every week. Part of the shock they're experiencing as they nervously glance at other group members comes from their long-held notion that substance abuse happens only in other families—certainly not theirs. Those in denial, isolation, and shock seem to be looking for quick answers and telephone numbers to call. They want someone to immediately remove their problem so they can get back to normal. They certainly need "normalizing," which is done by the group leader and by the fact that many others in the room are asking the same questions.

Anger. Those in *anger* have gone through the denial-isolation phase and are wondering why this sort of thing has happened to them. They recognize that their loved one is addicted, and they know that they should have seen the warning signs years ago, but their anger seems to have, at its core, a question of fairness: "Why did this have to happen to me?" When asked who they would have *liked* it to happen to, they're most often left speechless and with an insight as to the absurdity of the question. Veteran group members (those in *acceptance*) advise them that "fair" comes in only two types in this universe: "state fair" and "county fair."

Bargaining. Those in *bargaining* are trying to summon up a logical solution to addiction, though substance abuse is a logic-free zone. Thus, a group member in the bargaining stage may say, "If I faithfully go to Al-Anon meetings, and if I attend Family Week at the treatment center, and if I take good care of my physical, emotional, mental, and spiritual needs, everything will be okay—right?" They eventually realize that what they do to care-take a loved one will have little impact on the latter's desire to become and remain abstinent. The correct answer for this person is that if they take good care of themselves, it's certain that *they'll* come to be okay, even if their addict fails to recover.

Any group leader who asks an addict if there's anything a mother, sister, brother, wife, lover, or friend can magically say that will stop them from drinking and drugging will always hear the same answer: "No." I've done this hundreds of times, and I've never once heard an addict say anything but no.

Depression. Those in the group who are in the *depression* stage are often there because bargaining has not worked. Thus, they have not only worked through denial that their loved one is addicted, but they're slowly coming out of a secondary denial that bargaining will work. A therapist must certainly probe a group member for a history of chronic depression and should determine if the individual has suicidal ideation. If so, that takes priority, and most credentialed/licensed therapists are obligated under *Tarasoff v. Regents of the University of California* (1976) to report suicidal and homicidal intent (and suspected child abuse) to local authorities. But most often, what I've worked with at the FRC is situational depression, a natural outgrowth of anyone going through the grief process—whether due to death, loss of a major relationship, or chemical dependency.

Acceptance. Those in the *acceptance* stage become wonderful group members to have around because they're the grizzled graybeards of the tribe—they've been through all the grief stages and have become role models. They tend to their own recovery needs by attending Al-Anon Family Groups, and they help normalize the grief of each group member by admitting, "I once was where you are."

The Role of the Grief Process in Addiction Counseling

It often seems that what is ostensibly an *addiction* group can easily be seen as a *grief* group. I've mused many times during the weekly ninety-minute session that if someone were to audit this group or enter the group a half-hour late, they might find themselves wondering whether they had inadvertently entered a group that had grief as its focus. And often, when summarizing what I heard, I have asked the members if they are aware that they have been talking about grief.

"Grief?" they ask. "We've been speaking of how we're reacting to the alcohol and other drug use of our sons and daughters. How is this grief?"

"Well," I say, "let me summarize. Don and Kathy, you're here, admittedly frightened and bewildered, because your daughter Madison has been suspended from the best private school in the area. Soon after you found this out, and after

Madison admitted smoking pot for the last five months, you stopped having people over for dinner and you've stopped going to church and office functions in fear of someone asking, 'How's Madison?'

"Walt and Donna, you're here because Walt just got out of his third treatment center. And Donna, although he says it's different this time, you know that Walt has taken you down this dark road before, and that the result just might be the same. You're about to lose a valued thirty-year relationship with Walt, and through your thoughts, words, and deeds, you're already grieving this loss.

"And Dave, you been speaking courageously about your recently completed treatment for alcoholism, and you seem very aware that if you fail in this, you will lose your job, your marriage, and your health. You're in various grief stages over what's just happened; you're rightfully proud that you have made a commitment to get sober, but you seem to be going back and forth through anger, bargaining, and depression. And you are certainly showing keen insights into your grief over the biggest loss you've suffered so far—the loss of the old Dave, who once spent his evenings in bars and now goes to 12-Step meetings. You're grieving the loss of your old alcoholic self, Dave, and this group can help get you through it.

"And Susan, you are here seeking support because you're the daughter of an alcoholic mother who continues drink. You've married, have a family of your own, are successful in business, yet you are aware of a rather large gap in your life—adolescence. While other girls your age were going to proms and sleepovers, you were busy taking care of an abusive, dysfunctional family to the point that you lost your youth parenting a family system that was self-destructing. Most often, you're fine, but every once in awhile, on Mother's Day or your mom's birthday, or when you see an older mother shopping with her middle-aged daughter, you feel the pain again. Unlike your fellow group members who lost something a week or two ago, you lost something thirty years ago, and you know you won't get it back. What you may be doing, Susan, is grieving the loss of a vital parent, a role model, and the loss of your youth. You seem to be coping with this grief in a multitude of ways, including attending meetings of Adult Children of Alcoholics (ACOA), talking with friends, journaling, and understanding that part of what you may be feeling is grief. However, I can't promise this will ever completely subside. You may need to deal with this for the rest of your life. But you don't need to let it take over. Think of your loss as a scar, Susan. A scar is a visible sign that healing has occurred.

"So there's been lots of grief going on here. We begin the group talking about mood-altering chemicals, but we always venture into grief. We've all experienced losses of various types, and we're all in various stages of the grief process. Let's continue, let's read up on it, let's talk to others about it, but by all means, let's not be afraid to call it what it is."

So tacitly is grief mentioned in this group, so unaware of grief are most participants, so important to their recovery is knowledge of the grief process, that on many occasions I've used the Kübler-Ross grief stages as an "agenda round." An agenda round is used by therapists to break the ice that surrounds every group; more importantly, it is used to get a gut feeling of where everyone is regarding their feelings on a particular day. It's where the group starts its engine, but it stays in neutral until one group member takes a huge risk and starts talking from the heart.

When I first began to lead this group, I did a "feelings check" as an agenda round. I asked each group member to state a classic feeling word such as *mad, sad, glad, hurt, ashamed,* or *afraid.* This gave me an indication of who needed prompt attention and who might be okay if time ran out and they hadn't had the opportunity to share. I was trained to be aware, however, that this is not foolproof; it's not an exact science. Many who announced in the agenda round that they were happy, suddenly, 10 minutes before the group was scheduled to end, saw to their surprise that rather than happy, they were extremely miserable. Something about hearing everyone share brought them out of their long overused "happy shell" and into the reality of their pain. And conversely, many who said they were sad became relaxed, encouraged, and normalized by the time it became their turn to share.

When I recognized the key role that the grief process plays in addiction therapy, I experimented a few times by producing a chart with the familiar Kübler-Ross grief stages on it and asked attendees to tell me in the agenda round where they were on that chart. Don and Kathy might have said "denial and isolation," Walt and Donna would have said "anger," Dave might have said "a mixture of all five," and Susan might have answered "acceptance." Knowing where everyone is on this chart, again, is not foolproof, but it does provide insight into the grief every group member is feeling and offers the group leader some idea of where to start.

As in traditional psychotherapy, it's very important for all addiction treatment patients to understand the role of grief before they leave treatment or a voluntary process group. In fact, it's good to explore the grief associated with graduating or leaving treatment and to know where particular patients may be referred for aftercare. It is not necessary for those in treatment to have an understanding of The Truth of Impermanence. However, therapists must take steps toward understanding this fact of life so they may be better able to place the grief of their patients into a much larger, more fundamental "grief context."

5

Using Grief Stages in Addiction Treatment

> *Beth: I remember sitting on the front porch every holiday, waiting for Daddy to come home from work and crying because he never came until too late. So many holidays, we never got to family festivities because he was always drunk.*
>
> —Eric Newhouse, *Alcohol: Cradle to Grave*

Substance abuse treatment is a fertile field for dealing with the grief process. Patients and their families present for treatment grieving the loss of the mood-altering substance, the loss of vitality, the loss of a family, the loss of employment, the loss of youth, the loss of self-respect, and for many, the loss of spirituality. But few are aware of this. Like most, they don't associate substance abuse treatment with any form of grief. So patients must be taught that alcohol and other addictions (gambling, shopping, eating, Internet porn, and others) are all about grief. And not only is it all right to grieve these issues, it's necessary.

Treatment of Chemical Dependency

For instance, patients can be made aware that, ironically, addiction causes grief but prevents grieving. This is double dipping of the first order. As mentioned, addiction means one loss after another. During the first few months, the losses are relatively minor. A missed appointment with a friend, a slower-than-normal time in a 10K race, or a couple of extra strokes on the golf course. Then things start to heat up as the addiction gets more out of control. Relationships are lost, job promotions are given to more reliable workers, and serious health issues arise.

If you're a typical addict, by the time you seek treatment, there's been the loss of a driver's license, the loss of freedom to a jail of some sort, a wonderful marriage has gone down the toilet, no responsible employer will hire you, and you find yourself sitting on the living room couch in your efficiency apartment doing nothing but watching Jerry Springer.

Right about that time, you start thinking about the biggest loss of all—your life. You begin to think that everyone you know would be better off without you. You look toward the past and see nothing but deep regret; a glimpse of the future offers little but panic. So you begin to develop a plan for suicide that not only will get you out of your worsening situation but, depending on your life insurance policy, might also provide a few hundred thousand dollars to your widow and children. How convenient, you think to yourself—if I just had the courage to do it.

So it's clear that addiction is all about loss; indeed, the addict often speaks of himself as a "big loser." In a way, he's right. But he doesn't place all his losses within a context of grief. That's where a therapist and a compassionate recovering community come in. They can undo much of this loss by bringing the addict around to thinking of himself as a "gainer" rather than a "loser"—that he deserves to develop a fully functioning life in which he learns to meet his needs without substances.

But the other shoe has to drop—the one that says grief requires sobriety. Many addicts are startled when told this in treatment. A patient will mention that his beloved grandmother or grandfather died many years ago, and that he can't figure out why, now that he's clean and sober a few weeks, he recalls them constantly. He even dreams about them. He'll mention that he attended the funeral and wept as hard as anyone, but he still will not be able to figure out why so many people who are long dead are occupying so much space in his head.

The therapist will then ask the patient if he was clean and sober during their deaths—and won't be surprised if the answer is no. He will then explain to the bewildered patient that a person cannot grieve and use mood-altering chemicals at the same time. Like oil and water, they are mutually exclusive. This partially explains why so much emotional *affect* is produced during the first few months of recovery, and why the newly recovered are directed toward support groups that know postponed grief appears when abstinence arrives. Such groups will normalize as typical the grief that a recovering person is going through and will also assure the addict that he or she is not "going crazy."

Along those same lines, the therapist understands that alcohol is often used to self-medicate grief. Again, grief is all about loss, and loss produces pain and stress.

What better way for an addict to cope with this loss than to pop another top or roll another joint? During treatment, the addict will learn to cope with all his losses by means of positive coping skills such as talking about them, journaling his thoughts, and perhaps writing a note to those in his life who are long dead.

I personally believe, the Alcoholics Anonymous Big Book notwithstanding, that alcoholism is not a symptom of anything—it's a stand-alone illness. Resolve the grief, in other words, and the alcoholism abides. It can't be said that grief causes alcoholism. But it can be safely said, with little fear of contradiction, that alcoholism causes grief.

What else do we know about substance abuse and grief? Well, we know that unresolved grief is a major relapse issue. When a patient relapses, it is commonly thought that he or she may not be serious or diligent enough about their abstinence, or perhaps they are reluctant to attend treatment or are resistant to change. However, it could be because the patient has used mood-altering chemicals to medicate his grief. Many good clinics, when they encounter those who are called "reluctant to recover," often make arrangements for psychological evaluations with qualified psychotherapists to probe issues that remain hidden by the addict during his course of treatment. Such evaluations are often useful in discovering previously unknown issues, such as attention deficit disorder (ADD), bipolar disorders, and/or schizophrenia. They can also be useful in "outing" the various bereavements the patient is going through.

Patients may be forewarned during their treatment for chemical dependency that for a while after recovery begins, the various stages of grief (especially depression and anger) may actually worsen. Most assume that as soon as they go to inpatient or outpatient treatment, or even to an appropriate 12-Step group, that their anger and depression will immediately cease. Not always. Most of the time, grief issues that have long been marinated in drugs and alcohol work their way to the surface in treatment, and a clearer head also allows anger to bubble to the top. This produces even more stress on the newly recovering person, who may be tempted to fall back to mood-altering chemicals to make the pain go away. This results in relapse, and although relapse is one of the symptoms of the disease of addiction, it need not occur if the proper work is done.

Anyone who works in addiction treatment understands that addiction is all about a *bardo* state between *disconnection* and *connection*. Almost all addicts present for treatment having slowly disconnected over time from health, family, jobs, mental stability, and spirituality. Thus, much work and attention during treatment is directed toward getting the alcoholic or addict connected again with his health, his relationships, and his spiritual nature.

And it would be unfair to leave the arena of addiction without considering once more how *time* affects how we think of addiction. In *Outwitting Your Alcoholic*, I argue that because alcoholism is insidious, because its course runs over a long period of time, it can be called a disease. No alcoholic I've ever met took one drink and got physically hooked. Emotionally and mentally hooked, perhaps, but not physically. The usual course of alcoholism leads through *time*. Initially, small decisions are deferred to the drink, but as time goes by, larger decisions (Do I want my family? Do I want to live?) come into play. After awhile, they all converge into a calamitous perfect storm, and the alcoholic, it is hoped, enters treatment or recovery.

I'm still unsure as to whether addiction to highly euphoric drugs can be termed as a disease. This is not because I am chauvinistic about alcohol, my own drug of choice; rather, I'm aware that many other drugs produce euphoria (or a sense of well-being) so powerful that not much time elapses between experimentation and addiction. These drugs are so addictive that the word *insidious* cannot be used to describe the addiction process. Thus, for example, I wonder whether addiction to crack cocaine, a drug that packs enough euphoric punch to addict first-time users on the spot, can be regarded as a physical disease.

Substance abusers may be given information on the stages or tasks of grief with the suggestion that they develop their own study chart so they always know what state of the grief process they are in (see Chapter 1). At the very least, it will shatter the illusion that we live without *between* states.

Treatment of Other Addictions

Addiction to mood-altering substances is one form of addiction. But there are many others. Some, like compulsive gambling, are called *process* addictions because they involve an action or behavior that becomes, over time, compulsive to the point that quality of life is drastically altered. Certainly, Western medicine may one day find a gene or a specific location in the brain that corresponds to a person not being able to stop gambling once started. However, Eastern medicine would most likely see a gambler as one under the illusion that impermanence may be held at bay if a certain lottery ticket is drawn or if coins cascade noisily into polished steel troughs.

Likewise compulsive shoppers. These are people who medicate their moods by buying one more unneeded item and "maxing-out" one more credit card. And they can't stop purchasing once they start. Just as an alcoholic laments his debauch the morning after, a compulsive shopper brings her bags home, sets them down on the floor, and asks herself, "Why did I do this again? I don't need anything." The more astute will wonder whether she's merely putting off the notion that everything dies by grabbing at the discount table and clutching things from the sales rack. She may think, "If I cling to all forms of material goods and bring them home in copious quantities, won't that mean I have too much stuff to die?" Were she to be more mindful of The Truth of Impermanence, she might be interested in giving more of her material goods away. She might divest herself from the accumulation of things that will do nothing to postpone aging and eventual death.

Eating disorders might also be reframed to reveal an ignorance of impermanence. Compulsive eating could be seen as a spiritual hunger, or as the idea that developing huge amounts of body fat is a bulwark against the eventual coming of old age and death. Science may one day develop a pill that stops overeating behaviors, but it doubtless will do nothing toward a person's desire to medicate their way through grief and loss.

While relationships and compulsive sex are rarely seen in light of an addictive disorder, they certainly should be. Patients presenting for treatment who have a long list of serial partners or relationships seem to be taking people hostage, not dealing with their true feelings. Such patients seem to be clutching at people and tacitly asking them to keep them from pondering impermanence. In other words, if I have such-and-such a person in my life today, perhaps I don't have to think of the dance of death that we all must do alone.

6

A Lecture on Grief Anniversaries

o o o o o o o o o o o o o o o o o o o o o o o o o o o o o

Give sorrow words; the grief that does not speak
Whispers the o'er-fraught heart and bids it break.

—William Shakespeare, *Macbeth*

Introduction

Many good lectures are available that discuss the grief process in substance abuse treatment. I offer this one because it has worked many times for me, even in outpatient settings. Be prepared, however, for the potential impact of this exercise. On several occasions, I have seen patients become distraught to the point that they needed to leave the lecture hall and sit by themselves or with another therapist. "Blindsided" is the term they most often use to describe what they are feeling. Thus, anyone who uses this lecture should understand its impact and have a second therapist handy to attend those who are suddenly overcome by acute grief. The goal of this lecture is not to stir up such powerful grief; it is to ensure that patients see how they may be paying insufficient attention to a grief anniversary, to the degree that they ultimately relapse or harm themselves. I believe it's better for patients to encounter these internal calendar dates while in treatment than to encounter them later, by themselves.

The Lecture

Most of us are familiar with the special calendar days that are tough on those who are new to recovery. I've grown accustomed to referring to them as *external* calendar dates. When they loom on the horizon as Thanksgiving, Christmas, and New Year's famously do, a good therapist will spend a lot of time discussing them, especially in outpatient treatment where patients commute to centers several times a week. External calendar dates produce a great deal of stress, are associated with drinking or depression, and are *universal;* that is, all others in the recovering community share them. These dates are conscious dates; we know they're coming (most often, they're announced ad nauseam in the broadcast and print media). But even though we know they're coming, if we're new to recovery, we don't always prepare for them. As a result, we may relapse.

What a good therapist will do as external calendar dates approach is spend group process time ensuring that everyone plans for them. They don't want to hear a patient say, "Yes, I plan to sleep late on Christmas day, get up, and then hang with buddies all day." That's not a plan, at least not a therapeutic plan. Better that you say (and the therapist hear), "I'm going to get up on Christmas day, attend my support group, and then go to my sponsor's house where we'll all celebrate Christmas in a setting that avoids the pressure to drink and drug." Now that's a plan, and it's music to the therapist's ears.

Everyone knows a fairly complete list of external calendar days. It includes Super Bowl Sunday, Valentine's Day, St. Patrick's Day, Mother's Day, Father's Day, Fourth of July, Thanksgiving, Christmas, and, certainly, New Year's Eve. And we can expand it even further to include our personal birthdays, the founding date of the U.S. Marine Corps (November 10), and the pseudo Mexican holiday of Cinco de Mayo (May 5), known throughout the Southwest as "Cinco de Drink-o."

No one is surprised to find holidays such as New Year's Eve and the Fourth of July on this list. It's a time-honored tradition to make some noise on these festive occasions. And what better way to make some noise than to toss back a few drinks beforehand? You certainly can't watch a Super Bowl game without beer—and if we fail to think of suds on this occasion, our televisions will remind us, with many images of beautiful, young, happy people in well-lit bars, tossing back glass after glass, seemingly without impairment or consequence. St. Patrick's Day is so beer-soaked that it must pain many Irish to realize that their one great day of the year has somehow morphed into a national day of drunkenness and misery.

You may be surprised to find Valentine's Day and Mother's Day on the same list as New Year's Eve until you remember that all of us view dozens of television commercials during these special occasions that show clean happy couples and smiling families presenting gifts or Hallmark cards. And many of our patients will view these lovely idealized scenes as depressing reminders that their own families are long gone, or that Child Protective Services has placed their children in foster care. Or the fact that they have long been without a significant life partner and have no expectation of having one in the near future.

It's up to each patient to anticipate these *external* holidays and ensure, with the help of a treatment facility or a 12-Step sponsor, that they protect themselves by doubling up on their support group attendance and taking precautions to be in a "slippery free" environment that's free of slippery people.

Yet experience has shown me that in addition to these external calendar days, there exist what I call *internal* calendar days. These are the treacherous, often self-sabotaging days that we all have but don't tell anyone about until it's too late. These are *subconscious* days, unique to each particular patient. These days may include dates of trauma or of the death of a loved one, the date on which a child is given up for adoption or placed in court custody, the date a divorce became final, or the date on which a person relapsed and adopted a new sobriety date.

And certainly, internal calendar dates can be very pleasant. Your marriage anniversary, the birthdays of your children, the day you were mustered out of the military, and the day you got off probation, for a few examples. But make no mistake—until we therapists, sponsors, and patients actually have a vehicle for exposing these internal calendar days, they will remain coiled like snakes, ever ready to strike those we steer toward recovery.

Following the Lecture

The way I have learned to approach this lecture is to speak for, say, 20 minutes about the stressful dates we all share—the *external* calendar dates. And then I explain how we also have a list of *internal* calendar days unique to each of us. Once this message becomes clear to the patients, I give them 10 minutes to ponder their internal calendar dates and then come up to the chalkboard, write them down, and explain to the group why they are significant. It usually goes something like this:

> March 21 is the day my husband left me.
> June 8 is the day CPS took my kids away.
> September 6 is the day my dad abandoned our family.

It should be no surprise that this kind of exercise produces plenty of emotion, and it's good to be prepared for a heavy session by inviting another therapist to become involved. Don't be surprised if patient after patient troops to the board, writes their list, and weeps for a few minutes.

The Risks in Ignoring Grief Anniversaries

A recovering alcoholic since 1982, I remember well a "sponsee" who called me in crisis one evening several years ago from the transitional facility where he was staying. "Bill" (a pseudonym) had been making progress, had been attending 12-Step meetings, had verbalized significant insights associated with his drinking problem, and seemed on his way to full recovery. After I drove to the facility and sat next to him, Bill spoke of what had been a horrible day. The whole ordeal, he said, began upon awakening. He was in a foul mood, refused to speak to anyone, didn't want to leave his room, and essentially spent the day crying. So distraught and confused was Bill that he began to speak of his recovery in terms of hopelessness and uselessness.

Perplexed, I actively listened to him, but as to why he suddenly regressed in his recovery, I hadn't a clue. Becoming anxious, I suggested a full battery of psychological tests and searched my mind for psychologists and psychotherapists I knew. Then, seemingly out of my sleeve, I shook loose a quick thought: "Bill," I said, "today is October 24th. Does this date mean anything to you?" Instantly lifting his head, Bill stared at me and then said, "Oh, my God—today is the second anniversary of my brother's suicide." As we processed this, Bill came to realize that *subconsciously* he knew this but *consciously* was unaware. We spoke of his brother, what he meant to Bill, and he did his share of grieving. When we parted for the evening, he reflected how his failure to anticipate this important internal calendar date had nearly derailed his recovery.

The goal of uncovering and anticipating internal calendar dates is not to generate so much anxiety over each one that recovery is sabotaged. It is for each patient to recognize or anticipate his or her personal calendar days while still in treatment, respect them, share them with their sponsor and friends, plan for them, and essentially surround themselves with safe people.

I know a City of Phoenix employee who, each year on the anniversary of a fatal workplace shooting that happened in the early 1990s at City Hall, holds an "anniversary event." This is not meant to perpetuate grief or retraumatize survivors; it is meant to process what happened, to acknowledge the mutual grief, and to come together as a grieving community.

7

What the 12 Steps Say about Grief

The words *grief* and *bereavement* are rarely heard in Alcoholics Anonymous (AA) meetings, but that doesn't mean that significant losses aren't discussed. In fact, those who elect to speak often describe "what it was like, what happened, and what it's like now." In the "what it was like" portion, there is plenty of loss attributed not only to substance abuse but also to the fact that the individual wasn't able to grieve while actively using. Alcoholics also often share how they are inundated with other types of grief—grief they have *caused*. This is not only okay, it's necessary to allow them to grieve a terrible illness they didn't ask for.

While not mentioning grief specifically, *Alcoholics Anonymous* (the so-called AA Big Book) mentions one of the Kübler-Ross stages of grief. On page 417 of the fourth edition, an oft-quoted passage reads: "Acceptance is the answer to *all* my problems today." Acceptance of the disease and the harm it causes is dealt with eloquently in this famous passage (and elsewhere in the Big Book), but it neglects to remind us that acceptance comes only after a rather long process (according to Kübler-Ross). It may be up to the therapist or the sponsor to show a recovering person that acceptance happens only after lots of work, and that without careful attention and sufficient memory, acceptance can become forgotten.

The History of the 12 Steps

Central to all 12-Step groups (Alcoholics Anonymous, Narcotics Anonymous, Cocaine Anonymous, Overeaters Anonymous, and others) is a program consisting of twelve numbered steps that suggest actions a recovering person may take to get free, and stay free, from an addictive disorder. These steps evolved more-or-less from Christianity, most notably through the Oxford Group, a spiritual movement begun in the 1920s and 1930s by Frank Buchman, a Lutheran minister. Buchman believed that it would take a great movement of personal spiritual upheaval to heal the many problems of the world. As refined by Sam Shoemaker, an Episcopal clergyman, the Oxford Group began to assemble sets of *absolutes* (honesty, purity, unselfishness, and love) and then developed five *C's* (confidence, confession, etc.) along with five *procedures* for daily life.

Bob Smith of Akron, Ohio, and Bill Wilson of New York City, who in 1935 cofounded what eventually came to be known as AA, had both been exposed to the Oxford Group's methodological process of spiritual improvement. Wilson had been introduced to it by an old friend known as Ebby T., who got his exposure (and sobriety) through Rowland H., a prominent businessman who may or may not have once been a patient of Swiss psychoanalyst Carl Jung.

Many in the Oxford Group grew upset with Wilson's exclusive work with alcoholics. As Wilson and Smith began to eschew public prominence in favor of anonymity, and as the duo shunned the rigidity of the Oxford Group's spiritual dogma in favor of each person finding his own "higher power," the Oxford Group and this inchoate group of ex-drunks began to diverge. Bill Wilson put it best when he said, "The Oxford Group wanted to save the world; I only wanted to save drunks."

Once on his own, Wilson and others built on many of the Oxford Group's original precepts while adding many of their own, most notably, the ability of each alcoholic to enlarge his spirituality as he "understood it." As what came to be AA grew in numbers, the absolutes and procedures came to be known as the Six Principles of Recovery. Gradually, the number of principles (or "steps," as they came to be called) swelled to twelve. According to William L. White in *Slaying the Dragon*, an exhaustive history of addiction treatment and recovery in America, Wilson credited development of the 12 Steps to the Oxford Group, along with William Silkworth (a physician who treated Wilson several times during the early 1930s at the Charles B. Towns Hospital in Manhattan) and psychologist William James, author of *The Varieties of Religious Experience*.

The 12 Steps

The development of each step was laborious, with heated debate between members. In 1939, as the number of sober alcoholics in the still-unnamed movement reached 100, the 12 Steps and suggestions on how to work them, along with stories of the cofounders and others, were published in a book titled *Alcoholics Anonymous*, which gave the fledgling movement its name. Although none of the steps mentioned grief or bereavement, and certainly none were thought of as change states in the Buddhist sense, upon close examination, they clearly deal with states of *between*, transitions, and *bardo* states.

Step 1 deals with powerlessness over a mood-altering substance. When this is acknowledged and admitted, along with general powerlessness over people, places, and things (as mentioned in the second part of Step 1), it can lead to a disorienting and painful collapse of the denial system. This can come as a shock to those who are transitioning from unawareness to an inchoate understanding of powerlessness. Not only do we all live our lives as if impermanence doesn't exist, but we also live as if we were in full control of ourselves, our destinies, the actions of others, who gets punished for what, who should get punished but doesn't, who has a right to grieve and who doesn't, and basically, how people should drive their cars at all times.

This illusion is referred to in AA as "trying to run the show" and "self-will run riot." Perhaps the idea that we must control everything about our lives comes from something in human nature. Perhaps it starts with fear, and to keep fear at bay, we try to control absolutely everything. Or perhaps it's an old coping skill that got us through childhood and adolescence, but like most coping skills used by the young, it fails us in adulthood. Whatever the cause, trying to control all things and all people is a self-sabotaging act. Albert Ellis, founder of rational-emotive therapy, would say that the illusion of control is truly "irrational."

Thus, when those in recovery reach Step 1, they come into contract with the idea that trying to control people, places, and things is not only the height of vanity, but it keeps them frustrated and trapped in their addiction cycle. As they slowly emerge from this illusion, they begin to grieve. Why? Because they have just lost something central to their lives. They have lost an illusion, and they feel like suckers for having fallen for it. So they're somewhat shocked (the first stage of grief), and it's only in this stage that they realize they were trying to do the impossible, which clearly wasn't working. They see that the more they tried to control, ironically, the more their lives unraveled. Baby steps toward recovery can be taken after grieving this lost illusion and taking measures to ensure that the insight is never forgotten.

Step 2 is itself a *between* state, coming as it does between Step 1 and Step 3, in which a "higher power" is called upon. Step 2 deals with belief, which is but a bridge or stopgap between powerlessness and the concept of an all-powerful Creator. When they finally stop trying to run the universe by taking Step 1, addicts come to the realization that something far greater is actually doing the job. Taking Step 2 is very humbling. "Coming to believe in a 'higher power'" may cause grief because addicts are forced to realize that they're not the "higher power" they always thought they were. This may be especially tough on those who always lingered under the impression that they were God. Step 2 asks us to lose our pathological sense of self-importance (our grandiosity) and take our rightful place among the billions of impermanent, mistake-making children of the universe. Yet another shock comes when an addict notices that the word "sanity" is also part of Step 2. This doesn't necessarily mean they have been clinically insane in the psychotherapeutic sense, but it clearly suggests, as Carl Jung once pointed out, that perhaps they "kept repeating behaviors and expecting different results." Any alcoholic or drug addict can certainly identify with that.

Step 3 builds on Steps 1 and 2 and asks simply that a decision be made. If a person admits to powerlessness over chemicals and comes to believe in something far greater, it requires only a decision. Not a course in theology or a treatise in philosophy. Simply a decision. This collapses a *bardo* state wherein a person balances between taking no action and taking action. In fact, anyone who wishes to get and stay sober may want to make this decision many times a day.

Thus when a person new to recovery finally takes the first three steps, he or she has done a lot of what Freud and others called griefwork. They've discovered that they can't run the world, that they were driving themselves insane in the attempt, and they are starting to turn over their lives and will to something stronger than they are. This can mean a support group of addicts or something far more cosmic and eternal.

Steps 4 and 5 ask that the alcoholic or addict take an inventory of his strong and weak points. This can lead to profound grief as the addict comes to terms with the notion that he's shunned many strong points in favor of "character defects" (lying, cheating, and stealing) that led toward addiction and getting his own way. The grief comes when the taker of Steps 4 and 5 mourns the loss of old coping skills that, when reflected upon, led to loss of key relationships, loss of self-esteem, loss of physical health, and loss of independence (into prisons and hospitals). The loss of these character defects is keenly felt during this practice, but an understanding of all the ramifications of a willingness to abandon old coping skills doesn't come until Steps 6 and 7.

Steps 6 and 7, taken together, mean that the substance abuser is ready to permanently (as much as possible) offer up to a "power greater" the defects of character or poor coping skills he inventoried in Steps 4 and 5. The grief and fear come because the addict may, as yet, know no other way to get his or her needs met. This is a giant leap, a great risk, as the recovering person doesn't quite know how he or she is to go through life with positive coping skills rather than negative ones. Permanently turning your back on negative coping skills that have been used for thirty or forty years produces fear, loss, and a feeling of starting over—not an unusual state of mind for someone in addiction treatment.

Steps 8 and 9 are about making amends. Thus the addict is in a *between* state because he's losing innocence while making painful admissions and restitution to himself and others. He or she is grieving abandoned friendships, blown relationships, good jobs that ended much too soon, children removed from the home, and the hard, cruel words and actions he's dished out to any and all. This is certainly not to say that addicts are the only ones who do this. It's just that addicts who wish to recover must go through a somewhat painful process of putting things right. It may take an individual days, months, or even years to make restitution, and he may even find himself writing letters to those who are dead. But the amends are for him—they have nothing to do with how people react to them. Those doing these important steps may notice themselves going through various stages of grief, and it behooves a good sponsor or therapist to understand that working a recovery program produces grief—lots of it.

Step 10 is about making a daily inventory of poor coping skills so that the sun doesn't set prior to the recovering person making right what two hours ago he made wrong. This can be thought of as a smaller state of *between*, in which the person takes a daily inventory of his thoughts, words, and deeds. As he stays in recovery longer, as he becomes more adept at making these daily amends, he will notice that not much time elapses between the inappropriate action or remark and the making of amends. Indeed, he may realize that by taking prompt action, he can collapse a *between* state (see Chapter 11).

Step 11 is a mindfulness and meditative step, in which the recovering addict comes to fully understand that his or her life may be one great transition state. This important step can be thought of as a transition state because it asks us to reframe a negative act into a positive one. For instance, many recovering addicts may remember that not long before, they had opened each and every day with a negative affirmation: that they are stupid, careless, a loser, a bad son or daughter, or perhaps that life is a living hell from which there is no escape.

While in a treatment center or a support group, they can learn that they need to do little more in Step 11 than reframe their negative self-statements into positive ones: life is good, I'm in recovery, I have hope today, things might get better, and I can become, at least for today, a passionate, compassionate provider of all that's good in the world. Thus the worker of Step 11 sees him or herself in a transition state between negative and positive, between despair and hope, between darkness and light.

Step 12 is about carrying the message of recovery to other suffering people. It's yet another change state that gives us license to reframe a negative event (addiction) and use it positively in such a way that we help ourselves and allow others to grow as human beings. It boldly predicts that by working the previous eleven steps, we will have had a spiritual awakening. It doesn't mean that we'll see a burning bush or some sort of bright light, but our coming to terms with powerlessness, enlarging our spirituality, the making of amends, our abandonment of failed coping skills, and the enlargement of our spiritual natures will, at the very least, move us from the darkness of addiction (disconnection) into the sunlight of all humanity (connection).

A central tenet of the 12-Step movement is to remind newly recovering individuals that they needn't think of a lifetime of abstinence—they merely need to stay alcohol free and drug free for twenty-four hours, or less. "One day at a time" is how it's termed. Therapists using the so-called "abstinence model" of recovery have no doubt noticed patients/clients presenting for addiction recovery who visibly blanch at the notion that they may need to spend the rest of their lives drug free. This is bracing for all, especially for teenagers, who may not even be old enough yet to drink legally. In our model, this frightened client/patient is entering into a *bardo* state that is open ended. And like Viktor Frankl's fellow Holocaust survivors, this leads to the loss of hope in the first hour of treatment. What is indicated, then, is for the therapist or AA sponsor to remind the recovering person that 12-Step programs are not worked for a lifetime; they are worked for no more than twenty-four hours at a time. This collapses the open-ended *bardo* state into a manageable period of time, in which all a person needs to do is to stay sober and clean *today*. And when tomorrow comes, perhaps they'll do it all over again. Quite often, recovering addicts will forget this and panic over the idea that they may no longer be able to medicate their feelings. They will immediately feel better when reminded that they're working a "one day at a time" program, in which they need to concentrate their energy in the "now" rather than far into the future.

8

On Beyond the Grief Stages

o o o o o o o o o o o o o o o o o o o o o o o o o o o o o o
There is nothing staid, nothing settled in this universe.
All is rippling, all is dancing; all is quickness and triumph.

—Virginia Woolf, *The Waves*

Prior to a major Buddhist teaching or initiation, the Dalai Lama of Tibet will commission monks from a Tibetan monastery to create a large "wheel of life" known as a *mandala*. These monks, skilled in the fine art of distributing white and colored sand onto a large table, will spend days painstakingly creating a large, incredibly intricate sand painting that is visually stunning. Upon completion, the Dalai Lama will bless the sand painting, then strike several passes through it with a wand to begin the short process of reducing it to a few large bottles of useless sand. This is to honor and respect the Buddhist tradition of impermanence.

Contrasting the Medicine of the West and the East

While Eastern medicine sees no separation between mind and body, Western medicine distinguishes the two. René Descartes (1596–1650) was a French rationalist philosopher and mathematician whose ideas led to the so-called Cartesian notion that the mind and body can be divided into two parts (spirit-matter dualism). It was Descartes who asserted that the mind trumps the body when he wrote, "Cogito, ergo sum" ("I think, therefore I am"). After the mind-body split occurred in Western thinking, the body was given to the burgeoning field of science, and the mind/soul became the domain of religion. Thus, those in the West see themselves as tiny, discrete egos trapped inside bodies that are sole and separate from everything else in life (society, community, municipalities, and nations).

Western science and medicine mostly treats disease symptoms, it tends to be mechanistic, and it doesn't think twice about viewing the body as consisting of constituent parts. It's a very linear world where labs and molecules dominate. It's all about disease management, and thought is remanded to a physical process of the brain. Western medicine removes people from their bodies and uses national averages (e.g., formulaic standards for blood pressure and cholesterol) to make diagnoses. If a Western doctor visits a room full of people with the common cold, he or she will diagnose and prescribe pretty much the same thing for each person. In the West, there is a thick book called the *Physicians' Desk Reference* showing all available pharmaceuticals. If you examine the table of contents, you will notice an inordinate number of product classifications that begin with *anti-* (antidepressants, anti-inflammatory, antibiotic, etc.).

In the East, on the other hand, the mind and body have remained united and inseparable. Eastern science/medicine continues to be based on spirit, will, emotions—and last of all, the body. It does not think of the body as "parts" but as a living system that cannot be separated from its context or relationships. Balance is the key, and Nature is the boss. All phenomena are interdependent and related. Eastern mystics are not concerned with anything but a direct experience of reality, a nonintellectual pursuit best executed in a metaphysical or meditative state. Reality, in other words, is a nonsensory experience—it can be intuited, but it cannot be tasted, touched, smelled, seen, or heard. Eastern thought is where the West's abstract system of conceptual thinking takes a holiday. Were we able to use our five senses to divine the true nature of reality, they say, it would already have been done. Eastern medicine is circular, and strict attention is paid to individualized treatments. If an Eastern doctor visits a room full of people with the common cold, he or she may make a hundred different diagnoses and prescribe a hundred remedies.

Because I attend professional conferences related to addiction, I know all too well how Western scientists approach psychopathology. For the last fifteen years, every single researcher I've audited has trooped to the blackboard and drawn a "presynaptic neuron," followed by another figure that is labeled "postsynaptic neuron." Between the two is a "synapse" that looks not unlike the English Channel. Right here, it is learned, is where humans live—here is the essence of our humanness. If we are to address and cure psychopathologies such as addiction, depression, and other serious mood disorders, this is Ground Zero. This is, of course, predicated on finding the right drug that can duck-and-cover its way into an extremely complicated tangle of brain axions and change us from sad people to happy people.

Once these drugs have been figured out, managed care (or whatever system of health care succeeds it) will look to pharmaceuticals as the cheap and easy remedy for all our mental health needs. Western medicine will soon reach a point where drugs will be seen as the ultimate answer, and talk therapy and therapeutic relationships will be deemed quaint and useless. Once again, the reductionism of Western science, with its affinity for molecules and brain cells, will have trumped older Eastern models that treat the whole person.

The Buddhist Concept of *Between* States (*Bardo* States)

While those in the East may not have our scientific understanding of brain axions, they have many centuries of experience with how *between* states dominate our lives. These *between* states are all around us. They come from changes that are everywhere, and when we do detect them, we may describe them with words like flux, cusp, transition, transitory, momentary, mutation, juncture, pause, segue, uncertainty, becoming, waiting, intermediate, metamorphosis, transmutation, impatience, anxiety, suspense, ambiguity, fluctuation, transformation, gaps, spaces, crossroads, junctions, turning points, and "having the props knocked out from under me."

These terms describe notable states of change that enter and leave our existence like subatomic particles. Buddhists have long understood the extent to which such *between* states dominate our lives. Because these change states are so pervasive, and because we spend so much unnoticed time "processing" and dealing with them, they can truly be said to be major influences, if not *the* major influences, that human beings must deal with.

Physicists rightly point out that our visible world would look vastly different if the human eye could detect all the particles and waves that surround us. It would look different, too, if all our *bardo* states were rendered visible.

The best discourse about *between* states is found in *Bardo Thodol Chenmo* (a title mistranslated into English as *The Tibetan Book of the Dead*). It was written by the great Buddhist master Padma Sambhava in the eighth or ninth century for Indian and Tibetan Buddhists. In a 1927 translation, W. Y. Evans-Wentz used the Tibetan word *bar-do*, which means *change state*; specifically, the "state intervening between death and rebirth." So taken by the *Bardo Thodol* was eminent Swiss psychologist Carl Jung that he wrote a lengthy commentary on it and exclaimed:

For years, ever since it was published, the *Bardo Thodol* has been my constant companion, and I owe not only many stimulating ideas and discoveries, but also many fundamental insights.

Jung, it's worth remembering, defined the subconscious as positive and fertile—in contrast to Freud, who, tossing Eastern philosophy into the trash can of metaphysics, saw the subconscious as a latrine that needed a good scrubbing.

In a newer translation of the *Bardo Thodol*, Robert Thurman of Columbia University rejected use of the term *bardo* in favor of the word *between*. Thurman, a former Buddhist monk, wrote in the preface to his translation that Tibetans discern six *betweens*: the intervals between birth and death *(life between)*, sleep and waking *(dream between)*, waking and trance *(trance between)*, and three betweens during the death-rebirth process *(death-point between, reality between,* and *existence between)*.

Thich Nhat Hanh, in *The Heart of the Buddha's Teaching*, wrote that the Buddha taught about impermanence because he saw everything as impermanent. The Awakened One, wrote Nhat Hanh, became enlightened enough to understand that all matter will ultimately disappear—flowers, tables, mountains, political regimes, bodies, feelings, perceptions, and consciousness. Flowers decompose just as do people, he wrote, but that doesn't stop us from loving them. Nhat Hanh further wrote:

> Understanding impermanence can give us confidence, peace, and joy. Impermanence does not necessarily lead to suffering. Without impermanence, life could not be. Without impermanence, your daughter could not grow up into a beautiful lady. Without impermanence, oppressive political regimes would never change. We think impermanence makes us suffer…What makes us suffer is wanting things to be permanent when they are not.

Sogyal Rinpoche, in *The Tibetan Book of Living and Dying*, called *bardo* states "charged" moments. He explained that although the word *bardo* is commonly used to denote the intermediate state between death and rebirth, in reality, "bardos are occurring continuously throughout both life and death and are junctures when the possibility of liberation, or enlightenment, is heightened." He wrote:

> The bardos are particularly powerful opportunities for liberation because there are certain moments that are much more powerful than others and much more charged with potential, when whatever you do has a crucial and far-reaching effect. I think of a bardo as being like a moment when you step toward the edge of a precipice.

It can also be argued that, in *bardo* states, the possibility for potential and enlightenment are heightened. Indeed, Rinpoche wrote:

> This constant uncertainty may make everything seem bleak and almost hopeless; but if you look more deeply at it, you will see that its very nature creates gaps, spaces in which profound chances and opportunities for transformation are continuously flowering—if, that is, they can be seen and seized.

And the more our patients are taught to be sensitive and alert to their many co-occurring *bardo* states, the more internally prepared they will be for death of the physical body—the deepest *bardo* state of them all.

Incorporating Awareness of *Between* States in Western Psychotherapy

Remember "Barbara," the composite patient who presented for treatment in Chapter 3? Let's revisit her and see how a therapist who understands The Truth of Impermanence might treat her.

Barbara, attended by a therapist who is actively listening to her, says that she's feeling off her game of late—sort of bummed out. She's aging, her kids are transitioning to high school and work, old friends are moving to a faraway city, her father is in assisted living, her husband announced that he must soon make a three-week business trip, her purse was just stolen, and she's concerned that her job will be eliminated due to downsizing. Barbara adds that her mother died last summer, and that she really hasn't been the same since.

Barbara's therapist in Chapter 3 had not done his own work to come to grips with impermanence, so he saw only her flat affect and noted that she was probably grieving the death of her mother. A different psychotherapist, one with an understanding of the pervasiveness of *bardo* states, would see Barbara's life as an aggregation of many *between* states—the most noticeable and stressful of which, at the moment, is the death of her mother. He would see that Barbara is also verbalizing other *between* states. She notices that she is getting older, that her children are going through their own developmental stages, and that therefore her relationship with them is continuing to change. She might be ambivalent about this because such rites of passage bring news both bad and good. The good news is that her daughter was accepted into Stanford and her son has a good job with a local firm; by rights, Barbara should be happy. And she is. However, she may be reluctant to admit that these major changes mean that her home is without children for the first time in eighteen years and that her "babies" no longer require the mothering and protection they once did.

The close friends who she thought would stay five blocks away—where they have been for the last twelve years—have just announced that one of them accepted a better job in Canada and will be moving there in two months. This involves grief and wakes Barbara up to the uncertainties of life.

She also mentions to the therapist that she moved her aging father into assisted living. The therapist sees that Barbara, while perhaps unaware of states of *between,* clearly has on her mind the fact that the fellow who protected her as a child, who bought her a car, who danced with her at the school father-daughter night, is now eighty-five, living somewhat alone, and facing an uncertain future. And while it is flying under her "grief radar," the fact that Barbara's husband just announced a three-week business trip was both unexpected and undesired. "Why can't he stay home and teleconference?" she asks herself. "Why is our home life in flux like this?"

"Oh well," she sighs (always an important nonverbal clue to a therapist), "at least he's working. If my job gets caught in the downsizing that's going on, I very well may lose something I've worked for long and hard." She also mourns the loss (although she doesn't exactly use that word) of her purse, which was stolen. Rather than speaking of it as a *bardo* state, she simply chalks it up to the fact that the world is getting more crime-ridden every day.

The therapist, who has grappled with The Truth of Impermanence and understands states of *between* and how they affect all of us every minute, now sees Barbara's plight as more than simply stress or the death of a mother, but as a series of ever-changing *bardo* states, some of which are acute and need immediate intervention. He may then ask about other *between* states—Has she had a hysterectomy recently? an abortion? a miscarriage or a stillborn baby? Is she going through menopause? Are there any other major life changes that she may have forgotten or thought too trivial to mention? Is she approaching fifty, sixty, or any other age milestone? Is her health good, or has she failed to mention a lump found somewhere on her body that has triggered a transformation from thinking of herself as a healthy person to one who may turn out to have a serious illness?

After the therapist is satisfied that Barbara has cited all the conflicts she can recall at the moment, he might begin to see her as coping not only with grief from the death of her mother, but also as dealing with a large number of the *between* states that life brings us on a daily basis. He would not declare the presence of these change states a disease for which a diagnosis is needed; instead, he would normalize them, offer various coping skills to deal with them, and work with Barbara to understand, without overwhelming her, that life can be described as an unending stream of *between* states.

He might divide his notepad into two columns, one titled "Acute States of *Between*" and the other "Chronic States of *Between*," and note the death of Barbara's mother in the Acute column (see Chapter 1). This will require special attention from the therapist, and Barbara may be directed to a grief support group. At the very least, the therapist will want to know where she is in her grief stages. Under the column headed Chronic, he might want to list that she's no longer young, her children are growing up and out, her friends are mobile Americans just like everyone else, her father is now elderly, her husband will soon be unavailable for three weeks, and her own job is precarious. These may not rise to the level of needing a therapy group, but they bear watching and need to be noted, along with many other states of *between* that Barbara is completely unaware of.

The therapist could further suggest that she regularly make her own lists of acute and chronic *between* states so that she will understand, perhaps for the first time, how much change is going on in her life and how impermanent life is. This list should not scare her but affirm that her change states are just as real as those of everyone else—and that without change, life would not be possible.

Treatment Modalities for Exploring *Between* States in Therapy

Various treatment modalities could be used to treat Barbara as she begins to explore the many *bardo* states she's in.

Rational-Emotive Therapy. Albert Ellis views patients not as "sick" but as people who are troubled because of the "irrational" ways they think about events. One of the many irrational ideas that Ellis cites as common is: "The universe ought to be different than it is, and if it isn't how I demand it to be, I have a right—no, an obligation—to be miserable and emotionally disturbed."

Perhaps Barbara has irrational thoughts about the way life should be, and this has led her to psychotherapy. Putting on his rational-emotive hat for a moment, Barbara's therapist might ask her whether she expects to go through life without major and minor changes occurring often. If so, wouldn't that be irrational?

If, for instance, Barbara thinks that death and other *bardo* states render life meaningless, she might see her life as meaningless. If, however, she were to see that impermanence is necessary for life, and that states of *between* can charge her life with focus and vitality, doubtless she could summon up a desire to live and die with great purpose.

Adlerian Therapy. According to Alfred Adler, a one-time disciple of Freud, human beings are not simply products of what they are born with—they are products of what they decide to be. What we become and how we live depends on how we play the hands we are dealt at birth (existential therapists owe a great debt to Adler). In other words, we know in our heart of hearts what we need to do to be happy, but we often perceive ourselves as helpless victims and lack ego strength. If Barbara's therapist were Adlerian, he or she might remind Barbara that she is primarily motivated by social urges, and that her behavior is goal-directed and purposeful.

Adler saw that people, in general, are more affected by their expectations of the future than by what has happened to them in the past. Thus, if Barbara is helped by the therapist to understand the dozens of *bardo* states she is undergoing each moment, and that death is the ultimate *bardo* state, she could use this information to give meaning to her life. If, say, she were to discard the illusion of permanence, she would see the deeper meaning of reality; if she could ponder the ultimate loss of self and establish *time* as the central fact of life, she could view this as a strength, and in cooperation with the therapist, turn that strength into action.

Transactional Analysis (TA). A therapist fully grounded in the technique of Eric Berne might see in Barbara a "life script" in which change and impermanence are perceived as threatening and depressing. The depressive, fearful notions of her life script may have developed in her family of origin, where she may have learned that change is bad and death is the worst. The therapist could call attention to this, alert Barbara to the idea that the text of her life script was making her unhappy, and assist her in rewriting that script so that she could become a rarity—a person free of illusion and negativity.

And certainly, the TA therapist would congratulate Barbara for using certain coping skills to get through the traumas she may have experienced in childhood, while reminding her that these coping skills are failing her in the complex world of adulthood. Many patients like Barbara were successful in figuring out how to get through childhood (running away, reading and isolating, etc.) but discover in adulthood that these old coping skills no longer work. Indeed, the TA therapist might have suspected how Barbara coped with childhood by hearing her presenting symptoms; conversely, he might have guessed her presenting symptoms by hearing the way she coped with childhood.

Person-Centered Therapy. A therapist grounded in the person-centered approach of Carl Rogers might use non-directive therapy to assist Barbara. In other words, the therapist would regard Barbara as fully capable of understanding herself and of designing the balance of her life without direct intervention from the therapist. Such a therapist would first work with Barbara to develop a climate of respect and trust and then help her grow mentally, emotionally, and spiritually. Providing unconditional positive regard, the therapist might explore with her how fearful she becomes when confronting the many changes in her life, how she fears and distrusts these changes, how she seems overwhelmed with the number of changes, and how she has come to live in a depressive world because of it.

The person-centered therapist could build on the positive relationship that has slowly developed over time to ask Barbara to define the true reality of her life, and then to help her discover ways to reframe that reality toward a life that is both abundant and satisfying. If the person-centered therapy led to an awareness that change and *between* states dominate life—that lying beneath our awareness are the ebbs and flows of time's passage—Barbara could learn to see how change and *between* states can empower her to live with more awareness and self-actualization. Mind you, the therapist would not choose specific goals or outlooks for Barbara but would empower her to set her own goals. And once Barbara set these goals, once the idea of Barbara's life takes root, the therapist would empower her to embrace whatever she chooses to do.

Barbara would probably be surprised to find that her Rogerian therapist always keeps her abreast of his knowledge. He would never know something about Barbara's path that he kept to himself—any more than he would conceal some "technique" used to trick her into "doing something." A true Rogerian therapist would position himself with Barbara as an equal—a full partner in creating the life she desired to live. Nor would the therapist play a game called "when you take this action, I'll accept you." Putting conditions on a patient's recovery is considered non-therapeutic. This underscores the need for the therapist to take a closer look at The Truth of Impermanence and the states of *between* so that he may be of use to Barbara if she decides to dig deeper into the mystery of change.

Reality Therapy (RT). The core belief of this behavior-based modality is that patients need help in developing the psychological strength to evaluate their present behaviors and, if necessary, to change them. Reality therapy—at the opposite end of the time spectrum from Freud's multi-year analysis—starts with the premise that humans develop an internal, personal world and then perceive the real or external world in such a way as to fit their internal world. If a person's internal and external perceptions are congruent, then perhaps they become functional—they get their needs met and help others get theirs met. However, if a person's internal and external worlds are far apart, they will exhaust themselves (and others) in a vain attempt to insist that the world match their internal perception. Such "control freaks" typically visit many psychotherapists and often self-medicate with alcohol and other drugs.

William Glasser, who founded reality therapy in the mid-1960s, might have seen in Barbara a person who displayed passivity in the midst of all her change and loss but could learn during therapy to make the changes she wants to make. This technique can be thought of as translating talk into action. An RT therapist would spend little time with Barbara seeking answers as to why she's experiencing change and loss. If the therapist understood about states of *between*, or *bardo* states, he might alert her to how many changes are going on in her life every second, but he would spend the bulk of their time showing her how to make the changes she wants.

In other words, an RT therapist would set up a personal relationship that is mutually respectful, determine Barbara's strengths and attributes, strive to help her reach an understanding that life and all its change states place limits on personal freedom, ask her to narrow the list of changes she wants to make, and then hold Barbara to those changes if she shows signs of slipping. Of course, the therapist would be receptive to changes in Barbara's internal perception, but not to *excuses*. And he certainly would not ask or expect Barbara to try and change the unchangeable—time's arrow and the many *bardo* states it creates.

It is possible to see RT therapists as counselors who understand the concept of time, as they are most often tenacious about it. Although they are well known for providing brief therapies, they don't rush patients. In fact, if Barbara were to understand that her RT therapist is behind her regardless of how long it takes her to make behavioral changes, their therapeutic relationship would be further strengthened.

Gestalt Therapy. Fritz Perls was the founder and developer of gestalt therapy, although others preceded him in developing gestalt psychology. *Gestalt* (the plural of *gestalten*) is a German word that literally means *shape* or *form*, but it is also used to mean "a structure of...psychological phenomena so integrated as to constitute a functional unit with properties not derivable from its parts in summation" *(Webster's Third New International Dictionary)*. In short, *gestalt* says that we are more than the sum of our parts.

Gestalt therapists, in true Eastern fashion, treat the "whole person"; they do not see patients mechanistically as discrete bundles of reflexes, conditioned responses, and repressed conflicts. Rather than inviting a patient like Barbara to merely talk about what happened in the past or what is currently happening, a gestaltist would ask her to cease speaking about her stressors and to *experience* them vividly and immediately—to experience them "here and now" during treatment. After all, "now" is truly all we have. We don't have the past anymore, and we certainly don't yet have the future. A gestalt therapist would be careful not to impose techniques and interpretations on Barbara, but would wish to encounter her as a "fully present" participant. Only in this "here and now" awareness can Barbara see *how* she perceives her reality rather than *why* she sees it that way. If, for instance, Barbara showed reluctance to enter a therapeutic relationship or resistance to change during a session, the therapist would use this reluctance and resistance to create greater awareness.

Gestalt therapy places a high value on the ability of patients to deal with their problems if they become aware of what is happening to them. Awareness comes first in gestalt therapy, followed by patients taking responsibility for what they are feeling, thinking, and doing.

Barbara's therapy, for example, might consist of her therapist showing her how she avoids her troubled childhood and fears future states of *between* by never staying in the "now." The therapist will anticipate that Barbara, like all other patients, avoids the "now" because she's not comfortable in it. Her zone of comfort is regretting the past and fearing the future. Perhaps she will be reminded that talking about a problem is not to be confused with *dealing* with the problem. Fritz Perls wrote that anxiety (which can be thought of as a *bardo* state) lies in the "gap between now and later." A variety of exercises could be used by Barbara's therapist to "jolt" her into the here and now, in much the same way that a Zen master uses *koans* to jolt practitioners into new insights. The "empty chair" technique could be used, in which Barbara would either role play or dialogue with herself to discover why she avoids and fears life's many vicissitudes. Or she could be directed to a psychodrama expert who would show her how fluid, dynamic, and ever-changing her family unit is so she will learn to see and accept life's many changes.

Further, Barbara could be taught that resentments can be seen as emotional clutter that blocks awareness. Doubtless she resents the ephemeral nature of life and the many changes it produces. Were she to express these resentments during therapy, she would be well on her way toward reducing much of what Perls called "unfinished business." Her therapist would also be highly aware of her nonverbal cues, such as body language, facial affect, voice, movement, gestures, and the direction of her eye contact. This Perls called "psychosomatic language," and he wrote that it was a far better map of the psyche than mere words. In fact, Barbara's therapist might spend more time observing *how* she said something than *why* she said it. In other words, the gestaltist would pay attention to the *process* of her statements (her affect, her body language, and her insights) and would not get caught up in the *content* of her speech ("my son did this, and then I did that, and then his father said..."). He might draw attention to the fact that she often says "It's hard to..." and suggest that what she really meant to say was, "I find it hard to...". Likewise, he will be vigilant toward hearing the passive voice: "Many tears were shed," rather than "I shed many tears."

And last, Barbara's gestalt therapist would inwardly wonder whether she will be like most clients—not truly interested in getting well, merely wanting to become more comfortable in their neuroses. Barbara would be made aware of this phenomenon and would be challenged to steel herself for the often painful struggle that results in true mental and behavioral health.

Awaited: "The True Nature of Reality" Therapy

It is central to my premise that the essential reality of the human condition is that change is everywhere and that change affects us to a much higher degree than most of us realize—whether we like it or not. Although many of the psychotherapeutic techniques and philosophies discussed above call themselves "reality therapies," most never venture near The Truth of Impermanence. The world awaits a central philosophy or psychotherapeutic technique that takes an unflinching look at this deepest, most rewarding of all realities. Perhaps we could call this (with apologies to William Glasser) "The True Nature of Reality" Therapy.

9

Existential Therapy

o o o o o o o o o o o o o o o o o o o o o o o o o o o o o o
The future's uncertain and the end is always near.

—Jim Morrison, *Roadhouse Blues*

Grief is about loss (most often the loss of a loved one or a relationship) and how a person copes with that loss. The bereavement following death can be considered one of the biggest of the states of *between* facing any human being. How we deal with that loss has a great deal to do with the meaning we assign to it. And if there is any treatment modality that challenges its patients to find meaning, it is existential therapy.

Existential therapy has as its core the experience of aloneness, the search for meaning, and the persistence of anxiety as a condition of living. One has only to read Viktor Frankl's popular book, *Man's Search for Meaning*, to see how we all have spiritual freedom and independence of mind. Frankl, a psychoanalyst who was once a student of Freud, writes that regardless of what is taken from us (our homes, our personal freedom), we have an abiding freedom to choose our attitudes. The great Russian novelist Fodor Dostoyevsky put it even more plainly when he prayed that he might always "be worthy of his suffering."

It would be wrong to insist that existential therapy is a separate school of therapy or a well-defined model with specific techniques (such as Person-Centered Therapy, Gestalt Therapy, or Transactional Analysis). Existential therapy is actually a therapeutic philosophy, practice, or approach in which a therapist is both educated and trained. It values a therapeutic relationship far more than it values a set of techniques. An existential therapist shuns Freud's deterministic notions of repression, basic drives, family-of-origin issues, and primitive terrors; it champions free will, along with freedom (and responsibility) of the human psyche.

Without being pessimistic or antireligious, existential therapists ask their patients to come to grips with the fact that life is based on the meaning and the values we assign to it. It's there that we find a connection to the thousands of states of *between*, bereavement being the most powerful and the most visible. Frankl saw therapy as finding meaning *(logotherapy)*, and he wrote that the role of therapy is to help individuals find meaning in a life where meaning is most often hidden. Frankl hinted, however, that one place to begin the search is through suffering, work, and love.

One of the basic tenets of existential therapy is that human beings are finite and that life on Earth is brief. As we get older, this becomes more evident, and while we rarely admit The Truth of Impermanence, we do acknowledge that "time flies." In the *Rubaiyat*, a twelfth-century collection of verse, Omar Khayyam wrote, "The Bird of Time has but a little way to flutter—and Lo! The Bird is on the Wing." The older we get, the faster it seems to fly. Our chief task is to accept the fact that time is fleeting.

Another tenet of existential therapy is that awareness of death is a human condition. This is not seen as a negative thing; indeed, it brings significance to living. When we come to understand that our time on Earth is brief, we can clearly see that we must redouble our efforts to find meaning and to find salvation through love. In *Freedom and Destiny*, Rollo May wrote, "Our awareness of death is the source of zest for life and creativity." Only through death, life is conquered; only through life, death is conquered.

Yet another central tenet is that we have an ability to make choices. Existential therapists shun the Freudian notion that our subconscious is destiny; that what we do is predetermined, based on how much subconscious material we have in our brains. Existential therapy is based not on sickness, but on the wellness that happens when we discover that our discomfort originates, in large part, from our own actions. In this modality, mental health is based on how quickly patients discover the freedom they have—with the caveat that with this newfound freedom comes responsibility. We exercise this responsibility when we become aware that our life is based on the choices we make and stop blaming others for our misfortune. Responsibility means that there are consequences to our choices. Perhaps that is why Viktor Frankl suggested, in all seriousness, that since there is a Statue of Liberty on the East Coast, there should be a Statue of Responsibility on the West Coast.

Bardo states, as has been said, are charged moments of intensified life. There, one is always at a crossroads, at a junction, at a turning point. All these demand choices, and our lives depend a great deal on choices that we are free to make.

Patients determined to place themselves under the care of an existential therapist should understand that while they have freedom of thought and choice, blaming others for their lives is not an option. Neither may they stay in the grief process too long. In 1980, noted psychologist Irvin Yalom wrote, in *Existential Psychotherapy:*

> The therapist must determine what role a particular patient plays in his or her own dilemma, and find ways to communicate this insight to the patient. Until one realizes that one has created one's own dysphoria, there can be no motivation to change.

It is not necessary for psychotherapy patients to have an understanding of impermanence. However, psychotherapists themselves must take steps toward understanding this fact of life so they may be better able to place the grief of their patients into a much larger, more fundamental context of *between* states. Today, we ask current and future therapists to undergo their own therapy to better understand their personal issues, their personal prejudices, their personal fears, and their personal disappointments. I don't think that it's too much of a stretch to also ask them to describe the meaning of their own lives and how they deal with The Truth of Impermanence. Clients and patients of these therapists will not be comfortable dealing with the thousands of *bardo* or transition states they deal with every minute if their therapists don't recognize them. And if therapists themselves don't understand the significance of *between* states, they certainly won't look for them in their patients.

10

Collapsing the Bardo *States*

o o o o o o o o o o o o o o o o o o o o o o o o o o o o o o
Some are balls and some are strikes, but they ain't nothin' till I call 'em.

—An Anonymous Home Plate Umpire

In quantum physics, light is seen to have a strange duality. The light we use to illuminate our basements and garages, the light that we notice when observing the night sky, the light that is ours when a switch is thrown exists as both a particle and a wave. This doesn't need to bother us; in fact, anyone who fears for his sanity will do well to walk on the other side of the street, so to speak, when quantum physics approaches. We simply may enjoy the light and refrain from digging deeply into the spooky nature of the quantum world.

So thoroughly has the odd nature of light been explored by experimentation that we know (as well as we can) this particle-wave duality to be true. However, a deeper understanding shows us that it can best be thought of as a "probability" or a "potentiality" as well as a duality. In other words, light energy exists as a potential duality until an observer, usually a physicist, actually measures it. Strangely enough, if you design an experiment to see light as a wave, a wave is what you'll find. On the other hand, if proving the particle nature of light is your goal, a particle will become vividly apparent. Simply by observing light, a physicist *collapses* both probability and potentiality. This has dramatic implications, as it seems to place human beings both as observers of, and participants in, the universe—a chilling but fascinating notion that is well beyond the scope of this book.

Responses to Painful *Bardo* States

Likewise, it is possible to think of the many states of *between* this book has described as probabilities or potentialities. And just as a quantum physicist collapses particle-wave dualities by measurement and turns potentialities into realities, so, too, can a patient or a psychotherapist learn to collapse major *bardo* state transitions that are proving painful. Although these ever-present states of change happen to exist, we don't always need to think of ourselves as victims of them. We don't necessarily need to prolong *bardo* states, and there are actions we can take to make them shorter and less obtrusive. This gives us a certain amount of human volition and even rewards us for taking steps toward their minimization.

Going back to what we've learned about the grief stages, a therapist who sees her patient stuck in one phase of grief—anger, for instance—may explore how the patient can take direct action to become unstuck. This is not encouragement to hustle the patient from one stage to another to the degree that they fail to fully explore their anger, or to tell them they have no right to their anger, but it might go a long way toward empowering them to discover why they're stuck so they can move on to another stage. In this process, the therapeutic relationship may reveal that anger is a comfort zone for the patient, that anger is part of a patient's life script, that anger is masking the patient's fear, or that the patient has a pejorative definition of the word *acceptance* and simply doesn't want to go there.

Viktor Frankl wrote about this effect in his popular book, *Man's Search for Meaning*. Based on his experience as a Holocaust survivor, Frankl wrote that "man may survive anything as long as he knows when it will stop." He posits that many of his fellow sufferers in Nazi death camps simply lost the will to live because they saw their situations as never-ending. In studying those who survived, Frankl noticed that they seemed to have understood that their dire situation would not be allowed to continue forever. They chose not to wait for their captors to determine their fate, they determined it for themselves. These Holocaust survivors elected to take advantage of the "last of human freedoms" and chose their own attitudes. They found meaning in their state of *between*.

Similarly, the cofounders of Alcoholics Anonymous have shown millions of addicts since the late 1930s how to collapse the impossibly long period of permanent abstinence into an easily manageable 24-hour day.

Suicide may be thought of as the most needless, the most drastic, the most final form of *bardo* state collapse. Termed by many "a permanent solution to a temporary problem," suicide takes care of all *bardo* states with the report of a pistol, the leap from a cliff, or the taking of a pill. Many who kill themselves, if they were they able to teach us, would admit to having run out of hope after convincing themselves that nothing would get any better. Rephrased, this means that the despondent person found him or herself in a series of short and long *bardo* states so painful that death seemed the only logical conclusion.

Therapists may counteract suicidal ideation by explaining that states of *between* exist (grief, depression, and others), and that these states may be collapsed far short of suicide. Through mindfulness, forgiveness, and the taking of direct action, any *bardo* state can be dealt with appropriately. There's no need for suicide, which slams the door on closure. Ironically, it also creates dozens of horrible states of change for family and friends. Suicide certainly puts an end to a painful *bardo* state, but it also prevents a newer, more self-actualizing one from developing.

It's important to mention again that the collapse of one *bardo* state always brings on another one. The reader by now shouldn't be surprised that, like a vacuum, nature abhors an absence of change states. Suicide, for instance, creates *bardo* states among the surviving community of family and friends. It certainly produces an abundance of grief, and as we've learned, grief is the most visible *bardo* state recognized by therapists and patients.

Or let's look at another example. Let's say that a person commits a felony, gets sentenced to a year in jail, and begins to serve his time. He is determined to ride it out, and he does so without incident. In other words, he determines to take direct action of doing his time to the satisfaction of society. After a year, he has collapsed the *bardo* state of jail time and enters a new one that we may refer to as a *bardo* state of societal reentry. So it's not that we can collapse all *bardo* states; that is an impossibility. However, it's possible to collapse certain painful, depressing *bardo* states and enter into others that promise hope and recovery.

To offer another illustration, a woman who finds that she is pregnant enters into a *bardo* state that lasts around nine months. It's often far shorter. Seeing a baby to full term collapses a somewhat uncomfortable and often painful *bardo* state. Once the baby is born, however, another state of *between* emerges that, it is hoped, lasts far longer than nine months. The newer *bardo* state is usually happier and more comfortable (the adolescence stage notwithstanding) than the last trimester of pregnancy, and it shows us how we may, butterfly-like, put an end to a painful state of *between* only to emerge into one that is far more fun and fulfilling.

Or consider the Biblical parable of the Prodigal Son. A son receives an inheritance from his father and soon leaves the "fold." He leads a profligate life, then returns, as a humiliated man, to his father. After he left home, the Prodigal Son entered into a *bardo* state, and had he not taken direct action, it would have lingered perhaps until death. Both the son and his father felt pain until the son collapsed the *bardo* state and returned home. This, of course, initiated another *bardo* state (let's call it a state of *forgiveness*) that bore the fruit of reconciliation rather than the sting of separation and anger.

I need only to peer out my office door to view dozens of addicted people whose drinking or other drug use has led them to asking for help in the form of a treatment center or a 12-Step program. The long, painful state of change they entered years ago—when their chemical usage slyly began by solving problems, only to turn on them and *give* them problems—collapsed when they picked up the telephone and said, "I need help." This collapsed a state of pain and disconnection and led to another *bardo* state that can be regarded as a state of *recovery* and *connection*.

There are three major ways in which a person can collapse a painful *bardo* state. They are not new, but they are often forgotten in the descent into pain. Whether used alone or together, they function as a road map toward reframing a painful *bardo* state into one that promises freedom and happiness.

Mindfulness to Collapse a *Bardo* State

Mindfulness is a very old concept meaning the development of rituals, habits, exercise, meditations, contemplative activities, and daily affirmations to focus the mind on realities such as The Truth of Impermanence. Substance abusers must each do something every day to mitigate their chronic disease, much as those with asthma and diabetes do. If they forget that they have a chronic and sometimes deadly disease, if they do not stay *mindful* of it, they may relapse into self-medication and will come to no end of harm. Another term for mindfulness is *remembrance*. Many addicts return to their drink or other drug because they fail to remember, with sufficient intensity, their last debauch. Many others return to ignorance and illusion because they lack sufficient mindfulness to keep it at bay.

There is no single preferred way to develop mindfulness. Most use as many techniques as possible on any given day. Mindfulness may be had by simply speaking with someone on the phone; taking a contemplative walk, whether down the street or to a favorite spot in nature; reading an inspirational book; prayer; or regular, habitual attendance at a religious service or 12-Step meeting. An individual exercising mindfulness may develop a close personal relationship with a fellow sufferer, may ponder clouds or the night sky, or may journal thoughts and feelings. Just as there is no single approved path toward mindfulness, neither is there any single message that one receives through these activities.

Messages may range from a brief pause in the chaos of home or work, the pleasure of contact with a valued friend, or a deep, fundamental insight that is self-changing.

What these activities have in common is that they ask an individual to reach out or reconnect—whether to a person, a place, a sheet of paper, or a deity. And what is psychotherapy but writing and talking? What is journaling but a self-discussion that is put on paper and thus made tangible?

Essential to Eastern philosophy is the practice of meditation. Meditation is where all attention is focused into the inner self so that profound insights into the true nature of existence may be experienced. Those in the West use meditation to calm themselves and clear their minds, but Eastern practitioners often spend years in the practice of meditation, most often under the guidance of a meditation master. It is thought in Eastern practice that through discipline, the meditator will discover hidden insights and capacities that are present but have not been accessed. This allows a new freedom and the ability to visualize the sights and sounds in the death-rebirth *bardo,* which may or may not lead to a more fortunate rebirth.

Regardless of how extensively meditative techniques are used, whether in a Himalayan cave or in your spare bedroom, taming our "monkey mind," as Buddhists say, provides the health, happiness, and mindfulness that we need to get beyond illusion and ignorance.

All it takes to meditate is a relaxed posture, comfortable clothing, relative quiet, and lots and lots of practice. Buddhists use the term "monkey mind" for a good reason. Ask any meditation novice, and they will tell you that humans have minds full of thoughts that enter and exit reality like subatomic particles. They resemble monkeys in a zoo—forever moving, forever in action. Try to develop a calm, abiding spirit through meditation, and you will find unwanted, mundane thoughts exploding like popcorn. Try to keep your mind on love, peace, or impermanence, and you'll notice that you start wondering whether the trash was taken out, or if the dog needs grooming. This is very natural; when you become aware that you've strayed from your focal point, just refocus. It may take getting used to, but that's why the word "practice" is used so often. Keep doing this habitually, and you'll notice that you stay more and more focused. You may even experience a withdrawal of sorts when you lack the time to meditate in your normal manner. This is a *between* state, and you will collapse it when you meditate again.

Can meditation collapse a *bardo* state? Of course it can. Remember that many *bardo* states last as long as you wish them to. If a state of *between* occurs that is of significant magnitude to enter into our awareness, we may feel that we are victims of this *bardo* state and there's nothing we can do to bring closure. Although we may not be responsible for beginning the *bardo* state (that's up to the randomness, vicissitudes, and probabilities of life), there's quite a lot we can do to bring it to an end.

For instance, meditation may not seem like much compared with forgiveness and taking direct action, yet entering a peaceful inner world where insights are gathered is certainly taking a giant leap toward acceptance. Remember, a *bardo* state is a state of *between*, like grief. And according to the Kübler-Ross model, working toward the ultimate goal of acceptance stops the state of *between*, whether large or small. If one meditates in the traditional Buddhist way, the acceptance of life is most often the *subject* of all meditation. In fact, simply finding a cool dark corner in which to meditate, simply allowing ourselves to stop our head noise, simply seeking the calm abiding presence of inner peace is the very distillation of humility and acceptance. It is a reaching out toward an awareness that we are not in control.

Our ability to maintain sanity and live a serene life depends upon our ability to humble ourselves and make ourselves open to the notion that the world moves, as George Harrison once wrote, "within us and without us." By entering into absolute, pure acceptance, we collapse our *bardo* states—at least momentarily. Our acute states of change (physical, mental, and behavioral health issues) may require prompt professional attention. However, the practice of meditation will put a stop to the dozens of chronic *bardo* states and help us cope more easily with the large ones.

Forgiveness to Collapse a *Bardo* State

Another wonderful way to collapse a state of *between* is forgiveness. As with mindfulness, forgiveness is a choice or a direct action that can be taken. While it won't prevent a *bardo* state from happening, it will provide you with some control as to how long it lingers. Put another way, the change state is mandatory; its duration is optional. It depends on how much physical and emotional pain you can tolerate. Forgiveness doesn't mean that you've forgotten about an event, nor does it mean that you deny the event, condone it, or even wish to reconcile with anyone who caused the event. It is merely a way of working through a *bardo* state, in which you come away whole and cleansed.

The idea of forgiveness was not discussed much in the ancient world until a radical called Jesus of Nazareth first began teaching and spreading the idea 2,000 years ago. It is debatable whether Jesus was influenced by Buddhism, an older practice (some say yes, others say no), so he may not have realized that the revolutionary technique of forgiveness he taught was and is a great way to collapse a painful *bardo* state.

The Bible tells that a prostitute, who later became a follower of Jesus, was about to be stoned by a righteous mob. Thus she was in a state of *between* that was taking her quickly from life to death. This could have gone on for an extended period had Jesus not stepped in, made the mob mindful of their own shortcomings, and collapsed the prostitute's *bardo* state. This fusion of Christianity and Buddhism may be clunky, but it does perfectly reframe an oft-quoted story into one where we can see the impact of forgiveness on a change state.

A much more contemporary example will serve to illustrate the same concept. It appeared in *The St. Anthony Messenger* in the late 1990s in a story called "Oklahoma City Bombing: Two Fathers and Forgiveness," by Sandy McPherson Carrubba.

The story introduced Bud Welch, whose 23-year-old daughter, Julie-Marie, died with 167 others in the 1995 Oklahoma City bombing of the Murrah Federal Building. By all accounts, Julie-Marie was something special. Born seven weeks premature, she was given a 10% chance for survival but pulled through to become a talented polyglot. She not only developed and ran a children's program for Latinos at Our Lady of Mount Carmel parish, she also became an interpreter for the Social Security Administration in Oklahoma City. Julie-Marie was meeting a client when the bomb went off. Carrubba quotes Bud Welch:

> The first five weeks after the bombing are a blur to me. I wanted [Timothy] McVeigh and [Terry] Nichols hanged, no trials necessary. I suffered from temporary insanity. I would have killed them with my bare hands if I could have reached them.

A few months after the bombing, after he had gone through various grief stages, Welch asked himself, "What is it going to do for me if McVeigh and Nichols are executed…their deaths wouldn't help me one bit." As he more or less reached the acceptance stage of grief, he was surprised by those who celebrated when the death sentence of Timothy McVeigh was announced. "Vengeance solves no problems," said Welch. "The criminal commits a violent act. Then we, as a society, ratchet it up; we do him violence. Next, we ask ourselves, 'Why are we such a violent society?'"

Welch not only accepted the loss of his daughter, but his compassion led him to wonder how Timothy McVeigh's father felt. "I can't imagine what it must be like for Bill McVeigh. I'm not sure I could survive if my son had participated in causing death like that."

The September 1998 kitchen meeting in New York lasted two hours, during which there was a walk in McVeigh's garden. Afterward, Bill McVeigh, a family man who bowls for relaxation, said, "It's hard for me to believe a man whose daughter got killed could be that friendly and nice. He's a great guy." Welch said afterward that while he can't explain what happened at their meeting, "I feel closer to God. I'm not a real religious person, but that was an unforgettable experience."

In his reaching out to the father of the man who killed his daughter, Bud Welch was collapsing a *bardo* state. That particular state, one of the hundreds he went through during that horrible time, began on April 19, 1995, the day of the bombing. Had he not elected to express forgiveness, had he decided to keep his anger in the forefront, that particular state of *between* would have extended into the indefinite future. Yet Welch chose to translate his forgiveness into action. He processed what happened to his daughter and entered into acceptance. The acceptance he found led him to empathize with the father of the perpetrator; he came to see that the elder McVeigh was also a bombing victim, and he went so far as to arrange a meeting, and a relationship between the two victims was born. Thus Bud Welch, merely by thinking about and planning the historic meeting, collapsed the three-year-old *bardo* state he had been living and suffering in.

By forgiveness, one grieving father reached out to another grieving father half a nation away, and a *bardo* state was collapsed. Not overnight, to be sure. But little by little, insidiously, Bud Welch of Oklahoma City freed himself from victim status, began to express compassion to another, and came into the sunlight of forgiveness. One wonders what would have happened if all those who loved the 167 other bombing victims had the capacity to do the same. Then again, it's far easier to stay in a victim status, harvest the pity of others, and essentially stay stuck in anger. It takes courage to reject victim status, practice mindfulness, put Christianity into practice, and explore positive actions. Is it any wonder that few have the resources or the desire to do this?

If other victims of the Oklahoma City bombing elect to stay in anger as long as they live, they must periodically enrage themselves. They must invest lots of time and energy to keep their anger at white-hot levels. The more remote the triggering event becomes, the harder it is to get back to the level of original rage. This is easily explained by something called euphoric recall. Attributed to Vernon

Johnson of the Johnson Institute in Minnesota, euphoric recall means that human beings have a built-in ability to look back at a situation and remember only the pleasant parts—the euphoria. Said another way, rose-colored memories last longer than dark ones.

Psychologist W. Richard Walker, an assistant professor at Winston-Salem State University, wrote:

> When people look back on their past, the emotion associated with negative events fades at a faster rate than the emotion associated with positive events. People remember tragedies like folks dying, divorces and breakups, but the emotions associated with them lose their punch. The memory details are still there. What are changing are the emotions.

To add punch to his findings, Walker, along with colleagues, researched 500 personal diaries they had collected over the years. Their finding, which was reported in the 2003 *Review of General Psychology*, was that most diarists treated romantic breakups with a certain amount of dispassion, while other less traumatic memories (a football touchdown perhaps) were described with great passion.

Walker surmises that there is an evolutionary benefit from this. If humans were forever trapped in unpleasant memories, to the point of associating life with unpleasantness, perhaps humans never would have survived as a species. However, if we continually and dynamically reframe or minimize sad, unpleasant events into pleasant ones, we can get back to a level of happiness that allows us to move on with life. That's why it becomes more difficult to stay in an anger stage, even for people who vow to "stay angry forever."

Euphoric recall usually works by helping us get unstuck from negative experiences. But examples of how euphoric recall may work against us are legion. A woman may experience euphoric recall when she forgets the abuser she divorced a few months ago and gets seduced into remembering the good old days when he was exhibiting what is termed "first date behavior." This leads to the reestablishment of contact, plenty of promises that it will be different this time, and wham!—it's right back to ill treatment and domestic violence. What happened? She forgot the bruises and black eyes and remembered only the flowers and moonlit drives.

Addicts do it when they forget the last horrible weeks of their addictions and concentrate on the early days when their drinking and drugging might have been fun and solved problems. This leads to relapse and another round of lost health and lost relationships. Regular attendance at 12-Step meetings will enable an addict to recall with sufficient intensity the terrible agony of their last vain attempt to get high. The dysphoric (as opposed to euphoric) recall that this provides may be unpleasant to remember, but it will go a long way toward undoing the euphoric recall that W. Richard Walker says nature built into us.

One way to moderate the natural tendency to remember only the euphoria of the past is to ensure that we remember lost loved ones in a realistic manner. The cost of elevating a deceased individual to sainthood is the loss of their wonderful humanness—their flaws and other imperfect attributes. This is a setup for failure; no new emotional tie (marriage included) can compete with the exalted status of the loved one you recently lost. Understanding that people like Julie-Marie Welch were not saints and that Tim McVeigh was not the devil incarnate means that there are subtleties in life, and that nothing is quite as black and white as it seems. This leads to a clearer understanding of reality. An "inability to tolerate ambiguity" is a symptom of poor mental health (or delayed adolescence), and it speaks volumes to mental and behavioral health professionals who find it among patients.

Taking Direct Action to Collapse a *Bardo* State

The third and final way to collapse a *bardo* state is to take direct action. This prescription may seem to be at the opposite end of the spectrum from meditation. Perhaps meditation and direct action are the yin and yang of *bardo* state collapse. This leads us to believe that there's a time for action and a time for retreat; a time for doing and a time for not doing. This recalls the Serenity Prayer that is so familiar to those who attend 12-Step groups. Each meeting is opened or closed by attendees acknowledging that they lack the serenity to accept the things they cannot change, and they ask for the courage to change the things they can. And because it's often tough to tell what a person can and cannot change, they go outside of themselves in the form of prayer. When should I act, and when should I take no action?

If a person has used both meditation and forgiveness and would like to explore another method of getting out from under a *bardo* state, direct action is a tonic. Breathes there a therapist who has not encountered a patient who intuitively knows that action is required, but as Hamlet did, they feel powerless? It falls then to the therapist to help empower the patient to act upon whatever it is they need to do. If they are addicted, perhaps they need to pick up that 400-pound telephone and ask for help. If they are anxious, perhaps they need to be empowered to welcome a wide variety of options into their life to decrease this anxiety (talk therapy, pharmaceuticals, and behavior modification, for example). Whatever the malady, taking direct action, under the supervision of a physician, a therapist, a sponsor, or a spiritual guide, truly works.

And I've learned from my own experience as co-facilitator of a recovery support group (see Chapter 4) that it's important to explain to any patient, client, or recovering addict that merely talking about an issue or a problem is not to be confused with taking direct action. Certainly those engaged in treatment are to be validated for picking up the phone and asking for help. They are to be congratulated for taking a great risk of sharing their pain among group members they have never met. But all too often, those who simply share their problem feel better momentarily but forget to do the homework assigned by the therapist. In short, the anxiety that propelled them into a problem-solving group has disappeared, and they mistake this momentary lapse of pain for the sound, substantial, methodical work that all who desire permanent harmony must go through.

Often, taking direct action is nothing more than making a choice. Just as professional athletes tell us that their anxiety about "the big game" or "the big fight" goes away when the contest begins, so do states of *between* when decisions are made. I was acquainted with a couple who lived in Washington, D.C., for a number of years while the husband worked in the Clinton administration. During the voting debacle that began in November 2000 (a classic example of an acute *bardo* state), they were left hanging. They found themselves in the situation that if Al Gore won, they would stay in D.C. However, if George Bush won, they would return to Arizona. This *bardo* state hung on for weeks, with the predictable result that the couple found their life dominated by a huge state of *between*. Ultimately, they decided that they would return to Arizona, regardless of the outcome of the election. By the time Mr. Bush took office, they were in Arizona, had bought a home, and were getting on with their careers. Like those in Viktor Frankl's concentration camp, this couple decided for themselves when their painful *bardo* state would end and another more promising one would begin.

Our couple could have continued to see themselves as perpetual victims of this change state; however, they decided to take direct action and make the decision themselves. This is not to say that they were happy with all the ramifications of their move, but taking direct action did bring to a close a *bardo* state that they didn't consciously open. Sometimes we can shut down a *bardo* state by calling someone on the telephone; sometimes we simply need to go right instead of left; and yes, sometimes we must resign our jobs and move across the country. But it's clear that one may leave a *bardo of anxiety* simply by making a decision. This creates another *bardo* state, but perhaps it will bear tastier fruit.

For another example, let's say that you have a verbal disagreement with your spouse. You may feel aggrieved, family-of-origin issues may be tapped, your ego is in tatters, and from out of nowhere, a host of options spring up like weeds after a spring rain. You see that what you could do is use the "silent rage" possibility by not speaking to the spouse for a while—a passive-aggressive act if ever there was one. Or you could leave home for a while and take up residence on the couch of a friend. Or perhaps you could loudly announce to one and all that you are a victim and have been a victim since day one. Other choices include suicide or dissolution of the relationship.

Or perhaps you could consult a therapist or some sort of trusted advisor, sit down with him or her, and figure a healthy way out. In other words, you may adopt the option of assertively telling your spouse what your needs are—and take the time to discover her needs, as well. Then you could figure out a plan in which you get your needs met as a couple and decide to take a new approach to problem solving. This may be termed collapsing a *bardo of dysfunction* and entering a *bardo of function*. As has been said, a new *bardo* state will be created once the old *bardo* state is collapsed, but it might lead to both of you getting your needs met—a good description of a functional family.

There is a notable cinematic representation of how a *bardo* state can be collapsed. In his popular 1987 film *Wings of Desire*, German director Wim Wenders shows us two angels in charge of watching over Berlin. Cassiel is a consummate angel, highly professional and quite willing to hang around Berlin well in advance of civilization to dispassionately note the comings and goings of human beings as they slowly evolve. Cassiel is curious about humans but would never trade his eternal life for their brief *bardo* state existence. Damiel, on the other hand, is adventurous and risk-taking. He wonders what it would be like to experience existence as a human—to feel the heft of a rock or to bleed from a wound. He longs to know why drinking a hot cup of coffee and rubbing the palms of the hands together makes the cold tolerable. He wonders what love feels like, and he ponders the pain of separation. He's also curious about the concept of "time" and how humans can live their lives knowing that they will all too soon run out of it.

The most telling scene occurs early in the film when the two angels sit unseen in an automobile showroom recapping the day's humdrum events. Cassiel merely reports on the time of sunrise and sunset and observes, in drone-like fashion, that "today, on the Lilienthaler Chaussee, a man, walking, slowed down and looked over his shoulder into space..." Damiel, in turn, dutifully reports that a woman on the street folded up her umbrella while it rained and let herself get drenched, then added:

> ...sometimes I get fed up with my spiritual existence. Instead of forever hovering above I'd like to feel there's some weight to me. To end my eternity and bind me to Earth...to sit in the empty seat at a card table and be greeted, if only by a nod. It would be quite something to come home after a long day and feed the cat. To have a fever...to have blackened fingers from the newspapers...to feel your skeleton moving along as you walk.

Damiel has grown tired of knowing everything as a member of the universe's inner circle; he longs to trade that for the human experience of "suspecting" things but never knowing for certain. Seeking to end his long, open-ended *bardo* state of eternity, Damiel takes direct action by falling to Earth with a clatter and begins a new state of change in which he may feel, taste, hear, smell, see—and yes, die. This action creates a new *bardo* state, but Damiel vastly prefers it to the unfeeling, ethereal existence he has left behind. Damiel, in this fashion, recalls the Biblical story of Christ, but *Wings of Desire* may be saying that true happiness and immortality requires falling to Earth rather than ascending to heaven.

It's interesting that the waitress-turned-circus performer Damiel falls in love with explains to him late in the film that she, too, is in a state of change—from being trivial to becoming serious. In what she terms a "new moon of decision," she echoes existential philosophers when she tells Damiel upon first seeing him that, "I don't know if destiny exists, but decision does exist."

Once again, taking action to remove yourself from one *bardo* state will lead to another such state. But the cinematic Damiel seemed ecstatic to have traded a painful *bardo of yearning* for a more vivid, more sizzling *bardo of experience*.

Terrorism Viewed As Action to Collapse a *Bardo* State

As our post–September 11 society continues to grapple with the notion that more and more terrorists are willing to sacrifice their lives, we come to terms with another, extremely negative way to collapse a painful *bardo* state. For a number of years, perhaps stemming from our experience with the kamikaze pilots of World War II, we thought that a person's willingness to strap to their chest a 12-pound bomb full of plastic explosives, ball bearings, and nails had something to do with ideology. We suspected that they were all rather young, unmarried, poverty-stricken loners who had a pathological hated of Western values. It is more and more apparent, however, that this is not always the case. It's becoming obvious that when a nation or a community becomes stressed to the degree that it applauds abnormal behavior, suicide bombers will surface, if for no other reason than to be applauded.

This means that such bombers may not be ideologically driven but anxious to make right a life that has always gone wrong. Thus we see that those who sacrifice themselves may not always be doing so because of something they are fighting for. Perhaps they are simply reducing foreign policy and global conflicts to a personal level where they maim and kill for no other reason than their desperation to achieve something or to be fondly remembered by someone.

They may also be making a financial amends to a family that has been drained of all assets over the years as the future bomber floundered around, drifting aimlessly from one disappointment to the next. Through a single moment of ineffable courage, however, a disappointed person, who seemly fails at everything he does in life, can make a staggering leap from a ne'er-do-well to a glorified hero for whom dancing girls fling garlands and about whom the poets sing. His name goes on a list of great martyrs, and his family (who heretofore has regarded him as a disappointment) beams with pride and has their photo taken with some local tyrant. Thus the action of a so-called mad bomber can be reframed as the action of a hopeless person taking a direct, death-producing action that collapses what may be thought of as a *bardo of disappointment*.

The action is further replicated when other disappointed men and women see the adulation in the media, and the seed is sown for their own leap from obscurity to godlike status. Is it any wonder that disaffected suicide bombers are an economically viable and cost-effective way for fringe groups to get their message across? They need absolutely no training, and their single moment of courage shatters buses, bodies, and our carefully crafted illusion of security.

Taking Sides to Collapse a *Bardo* State

While it may not be elevated to the level of the three primary ways of collapsing a *bardo* state (mindfulness, forgiveness, and direct action), a case can be made for stopping and starting *bardo* states simply by choosing sides. Regardless of how it's termed (e.g., "taking a stand," "choosing a position"), it's clear that once we burn our ships as did those in Troy, once we cross the Rubicon as did Caesar, once we leap that line drawn in the dirt as did those at the Alamo, we immediately collapse certain *bardo* states and begin others. Many live their lives under the illusion that to protect themselves, they must never take a position on anything. Their ambiguousness seems, stealth-like, to allow them to fly under the radar of life where they never, ever, need call attention to themselves by taking a position.

There is a price to pay for this. A person who never takes a position lives perpetually in a *bardo of becoming;* he or she will never know what it feels like to live in a *bardo of action* or *attainment.* Toward the end of such a life, the person who can't make choices seems to drown, to choke, on his or her own possibilities. States of change are tough, but we spurn them at our peril. The idea is to see change states, understand how they affect us, get comfortable with the idea that their numbers are legion, and to adopt coping skills that allow us to roll with them. Not to decide, as the psychotherapist once said, is to decide.

Dreams and Reality

A few years after he made his famous "I Have a Dream" speech in late August of 1963, the Reverend Martin Luther King Jr. gave a filmed interview, during which he admitted that although his dream of a race-less America was eloquent, reality was falling farther and farther behind that vision. It was easier to desegregate a lunch counter, he said, than to address the social injustice and poverty that continued to plague Black America. Dreams are great, he seemed to say, but they collapse at the point where reality creeps in.

He probably didn't realize how right he was. Not only do dreams die when reality sets in, but they *must* die so that reality can occur. A pleasant *bardo of possibility* will always vanish when a painful *bardo of reality* appears. Three classic examples show how dreams vanish once a decision needs to be made. Two of them appeared mere inches from each other on the front page of the *New York Times* on August 31, 2003.

The first was headlined, "Concern Growing As Families Bypass 9/11 Victims' Fund." The families and loved ones of those who died on September 11 at the World Trade Center site, at the Pentagon, and on United Flight 93 were eligible for up to $3 billion from a special fund made possible by thousands of generous Americans. This fund would be used, among other things, to educate children of the victims, with the amount offered survivors corresponding to the victim's financial "worth." It was expected that all eligible survivors would sign up for this fund because, after all, they deserved it. This was a financial *bardo of opportunity* created not long after the tragedy, and it was statutorily set to expire on December 22, 2003, about four months from when the news article appeared. The article reported that, almost two years after the horrific events, about 60% of victim families had not filed claims with the victim compensation fund. Experts who pondered this situation surmised that some shunned the fund because it demanded that all litigation be deflected from the airlines and directed toward a terrorist or a terrorist group. Others may have decided to hold out awaiting developments in a federal lawsuit. Still others declined payment because it would force them to end a *bardo of hope* and enter a *bardo of reality*. That is to say, some grieving victims who once dreamed of a just compensation seemed unable to tap the fund because it meant painful memories, mountains of paperwork, and ultimate acceptance that their loved one was truly dead. I suspect, however, that there is also a fourth reason—that actually securing cash from the fund would collapse a dream. That as compensation came closer to being a reality, the survivors began to see that no price could be put on the value of a human being. That regardless of how much money they were to receive, the loved one wasn't coming back. As long as they could fantasize that the fund would make the pain of September 11 go away, the families expressed an interest. As the two-year deadline approached, however, they began to see this fantasy unravel. Exit dream, enter reality.

The second example ("Now Free to Marry, Canada's Gays Say, 'Do I?'") reported the fact that on June 10, 2003, Ontario's highest court had extended marriage rights to same-sex couples. Thousands of gays and lesbians wept with joy as this decision came over the television news, just as they had a few weeks later in America when the U.S. Supreme Court removed barriers to gay unions. Yet when it came time to line up for the actual marriages, there were few takers. So, what happened?

Like those who lost family members on 9/11, the dream of gay marriage was stronger than its reality. As wedding chapels finally opened to them, many in committed gay relationships suddenly feared that their *bardo of possibility* would be collapsed by a new state of change wherein commitment was not just hinted at, but legally binding. Fearing the fidelity promise (a custom honored more in the breach than the observance by many straight couples) and the "till death do us part" provisions of traditional weddings, many gays, it seems, liked the dream better than the reality and were loath to collapse it with vows, rings, and legal documents.

And the third example of how *bardos of possibility* are preferred over *bardos of reality* lies within the prosaic, pasteboard confines of a lottery ticket. Anyone who knows about gambling can tell you that lottery or Powerball tickets, while certainly part of the overall gambling experience, are nevertheless unique. If you play blackjack, video poker, or keno in coffee shops, you place your bets with a certain amount of hope—perhaps you'll leave Las Vegas or Atlantic City a big winner, and voila, all your financial problems will be solved—but these dreams are miniscule compared to the dreams of those who buy lottery tickets.

Lottery and Powerball ticket holders have lots of time to fantasize about their winnings. Those who spin the roulette wheel or shoot craps have time for only a little fantasy—mostly, they're too busy playing the game. Lottery players buy their Powerball tickets days and sometimes weeks before a number is drawn for the $250 million prize. And how do they spend the intervening time? By dreaming about what they'll do with their winnings. They have plenty of time to picture themselves on their own South Seas island with their own fleet of yachts. They look out the window of their home and see a large, fully equipped Winnebago sitting where an old truck is now perched up on blocks. Or they see themselves forsaking their small house for a mansion that overlooks a scenic bay and the houses of those who once oppressed or shamed them.

Anytime the owner of a lottery ticket starts feeling depressed, all she needs to do is look at her ticket. Never mind that the odds of winning are 25,000,000 to 1; she sees in that small piece of paper a way out of a painful, humdrum existence. Once the winning number is called, once a choice is made and a lucky winner emerges, the ticket becomes worthless, the dream is shattered, and the *bardo of possibility* is collapsed. That is, until another ticket is purchased that brings fantasy back to the purchaser.

Being Too Hasty in Collapsing a *Bardo* State

We now see that there are many ways to conclude a negative *bardo* state and to introduce into our lives a more positive, more fulfilling one. And indeed, we've seen that some of us permanently stop a state of change through self-destruction, whether in a lonely room or, plastic explosive strapped to our chest, in a crowd of people. So perhaps we should also be aware that when it's time to call a halt to a *bardo* state, we can be too hasty. As with comedy, timing is everything.

Before I provide two examples of how anxiety can propel us to over-zealously make an ill-timed decision, let me point out that being too hasty about making a decision can render us satisfied about ending one *bardo* state but ill-equipped to face a new one. In other words, we know we can make changes in our lives, but is the change necessarily being done at the right time? Are we simply trading one grief for a brand new and even bigger one? Are we trading the devil we know for the devil we don't?

I have, over the years, encountered patients who are grief-stricken over the death of a family pet. So beloved was this pet that it was given an honorary place on the family tree. Before its death, this pet had provided the children of the family with a delightful companion, but by the time they became adolescents, the pet was clearly in old age. After the death of the cat or dog, the family began to grieve—a must no matter how old the pet, no matter how the pet died. However, on its way to the acceptance stage of the Kübler-Ross grief model, the family entered the anger and depression stages. This became too much for the parents to bear, and like an addict who treats withdrawal with another dose of the offending chemical, they buy another pet. In other words, they fail to go through the stages of grief (in anyone's model) and try to short-circuit the grief process with a trip to the pet store.

Now, with new pet in hand, they can't figure out why they continue to cry over the dead pet. Perhaps it's because the interrupted grief cycle will not be denied simply because a different animal is in the house. Perhaps they were successful in collapsing a *bardo of grief* but were totally unprepared—emotionally, mentally, and physically—to handle the new *bardo* state that appeared in its place.

Regrettably, this is not a syndrome associated only with pet owners. How many times has the reader been shocked to find a widowed friend dealing with the death of a spouse by remarrying in what was once termed "unseemly haste"? Shakespeare's Hamlet saw his mother wed again so quickly after his father's murder that the "funeral baked meats did coldly furnish forth the marriage table." So it seems that many people deal with the loss of a partner by quickly entering into a new relationship. Like the pet owner, this seems an easier, softer way, but like most easy paths, danger lurks right around the corner. Far better to do the griefwork first, and then make new attachments. Far better to use the grief stages to collapse a *bardo of suffering* prior to entering new entanglements. Far better to mourn the loss of an addiction through a support group than grab hold of a new addiction that takes one to exactly the same painful place.

The same principle holds true for those who are in a state of change over their jobs. Every therapist knows a client or patient who is anxious about a good job that is quickly going south. The patient will mention that the job has been held over a long period of time, but that changes at the corporate level, or a new supervisor with whom the client is at odds, is causing a lot of stress. The facial expressions of the client will brighten as she explains that she's reading the want ads every day, looking for greener pastures and better working conditions. Said another way, they are anxiously looking for a way to collapse the painful *bardo* state they're in. This is attempted so often that most therapists encounter what may be termed as "serial job-seekers," who go from job to job in an effort to find one that does not demand emotional flexibility.

Certainly, searching for and finding a new job can be thought of as one way to take direct action toward collapsing a painful *bardo* state. It certainly beats taking a gun to work. However, a therapist worth his or her salt will mention that finding a job that doesn't feature a degree of stress may be one of those "irrational" ideas that Albert Ellis warns us against. And the therapist can also probe the patient as to why she goes from job to job. Is it because she might not have enough coping skills to roll with the punches, make the necessary changes, and cope with the ups and downs that the workaday world involves? The therapist may then challenge the patient to develop a skill set that will allow her to grieve changes in the workplace and find enough acceptance to continue as a productive member of a firm or corporation. Simply fleeing a job or a marriage by grasping at any straw that comes along is collapsing one painful *bardo* state in favor of an even more painful one.

Foot-Dragging in Collapsing a *Bardo* State

Just as we have seen that it's quite possible to be too hasty in collapsing a *bardo* state, it's obvious that many will needlessly prolong one. For example, parental pressure is often needed to make us do our homework. A college counselor often collapses a *bardo of possibility* by insisting that it's time to declare a major. A nudge from the judge is often what it takes to get us into recovery from alcoholism after a long list of drunk driving tickets. Wives, it's been observed, are most often needed to finally dispose of a husband's shoes that are decades old and, though comfortable, are falling apart.

Psychotherapists can help us find why we lack empowerment to change. Ministers, priests, and rabbis are often consulted about confusion in matters of conscience and spirit. They are agents of change and can help us quickly convert foot dragging into a race toward mental and behavioral health.

As William F. Buckley Jr. once observed, "We are liberated by deadlines." Give a wordsmith an assignment, and he or she may sit there forever with a blank look and a blank computer screen. Give them the expected number of words and a deadline, however, and watch their fingers fly.

Regarding more serious matters—death, for instance—societal conventions and admonitions may force some into taking action that they would not ordinarily take. When a person loses a spouse or great friend to death, a combination of societal norms, legal requirements, and spiritual practices automatically kick in to deal with this *bardo of becoming*. Friends comfort the bereaved, some contact the funeral home, some oversee delivery of the body to the mortuary, others write the obituary, and plans are drawn for the text and music of the funeral. After a few days (far fewer if you are Jewish or Muslim), a memorial service takes place, and the remains are situated in their final resting place. Thus, even while the surviving family members are distracted by the grief stages, the process of death goes on and the post-funeral activities (thank-you notes, property distribution, etc.) begin. One needs only to encounter a death in the family to notice how well, how smoothly, how magically, this all takes place.

It's exactly this type of compassionate pressure that makes a memorial service work. What would happen to grievers if this did not automatically take place? I suspect that for many, the experience of profound grief might render them completely unable to take direct action. Thus, the funeral process would grind to a halt, memorial services would be in complete disarray, and bodies would stack up at mortuaries.

So it seems that while some rush to collapse *bardo* states with unseemly haste, others need deadlines and pressures to accomplish anything. Remember the grieving family members who had two years to file for the special victims' fund established not long after September 11? After two years, many stated that they weren't yet ready to fill out the paperwork. How long is needed—another two years? twenty years? Is it possible that such people might never take direct action on this painful matter unless they are forced to by federal authorities? Deadlines and other pressures liberate us from open-ended *bardos*. They establish an arbitrary time for us to make a decision that otherwise may never have been made. Some, in other words, can't wait to collapse a *bardo* state—while others simply must be pushed.

11

The Rewards of Bardo *Knowledge*

○ ○

We do not know where death awaits, so let us wait for it everywhere.

—Michel de Montaigne

Now that we know how the practice of meditation, forgiveness, and direct action (practiced singularly or in combination) can collapse the *bardo* states that plague us and propel us into less painless, more affirming, more promising states of *between*, what do we get for our efforts? Why should we place change and impermanence into the forefront of our lives? Why should we spend time affirming that someday we will cease to exist?

Clarification of Life's Priorities

First, we will find that our *bardo* knowledge provides us with a better understanding of how many *between* states we are experiencing at any given moment. We can then reframe them to move us from a lifetime that is meaningless to one that is meaningful.

We all claim to be stressed, for example—we have schedules to meet, obligations to keep, and our big and not-so-big jobs. These allow us to keep our cars, our homes, and the creature comforts that we're accustomed to. So the word we often hear when we ask our friends how they are is the word *busy*. This is most often said automatically and with little forethought. We don't think about it, the word just pops out. Forty years ago, we might have answered the question with the word *fine*. The hectic life we all lead in the new millennium, however, has slowly replaced the word *fine* with *busy*. We live with schedules our computers arrange for us and with text messaging, cell phones, beepers, and pagers, and we have noisy and instant access to everyone, to the degree that our friends and coworkers express annoyance if they must wait more than thirty seconds to reach us.

Using the word *busy* after a polite inquiry may also be a boast. It seems that we are hurtling around, hustling our children to dance classes and sports competitions, and working huge amounts of overtime to such an extent that if we don't mention to our inquiring friends that we are stretched to the max, it may appear that we're lazy and falling behind. And that's something most people these days will not admit to. The word *busy* implies to our friends that we're not slackers. We're getting ahead, we have huge mortgages, we barely see our family members, and both our kids have been working to get into Stanford or Yale since they were four years old.

So yes, we're busy. But being aware of all the states of change we're in at any given moment, understanding The Truth of Impermanence, could allow us to replace the word *busy* with the phrase *ever-changing*. Imaging how shocked our friends would be, the next time they inquire about us, to hear us reply, "Ever-changing." Understanding how ephemeral our lives are would elevate our thoughts and lead to an awareness that life is short and that our mere rushing around creates nothing but more rushing around. Saying the word *busy* teaches us nothing; in fact, it might just be depressing us. However, it is impossible to use the words *ever-changing* without overhearing ourselves and putting our priorities and perspectives in the correct order. The words *ever-changing* could become a mantra that we use twenty times a day to increase our awareness of the hugeness of life and the small part we each play in it.

Understanding Impermanence As Promise

Second, understanding our many *bardo* states allows us to reframe *impermanence* as *promise*. Remember in an earlier chapter when I lamented that the word *grief* is so synonymous with *death* that perhaps we need a new word? I think that word is *promise*. Thus, The Truth of Impermanence may be thought of as the *bardo of promise* or the *bardo of hope*. Change, it should be remembered, is neither good nor bad. All animals undergo change, but only humans, with their well-developed cerebral cortex, use highly charged words like *dreadful* and *horrible* to describe it. If we learned to reframe impermanence without denying its existence, impermanence and change could also be thought of as awe-inspiring, wonderful, and affirming.

Greater Awareness of Living

Third, the reward we get for tackling impermanence is the awareness that only through death does life have meaning. Remember that the existential therapists teach us that life has the meaning that we assign to it? This means that life doesn't come with meaning attached to it like a tag on a new mattress. No person on Earth arrives in the hospital delivery room with a computer printout showing how their new life is to be lived. No, it's up to us to find it. Sadly, many find little meaning in their lives, and their day-to-day existence becomes bleak and depressive. Others, however, live lives full of compassion, love, self-sacrifice, and an expanded spirituality. And to fully embrace life is to fully embrace impermanence and all its ramifications. While Buddhists meditate on the nature of impermanence to rehearse for a more fortunate rebirth, all others may use it to maximize our time in service to ourselves and others.

Acceptance of Physical Death

Fourth, accepting the impermanence of life will speed us on the way toward accepting physical death. Dealing with states of *between* during life can be thought of as rehearsal for death. Those in the East believe that the thought of death should be on everyone's mind at all times. The Dalai Lama of Tibet spends much of his time meditating about his death and the choices he needs to make during the death-rebirth process. Only by rehearsing for death can we (and he) calmly face the end of life as we know it. To do otherwise is to go into this natural process afraid and alone. Dying is not the worst thing that can happen; the worst thing that can happen is to handle it poorly.

Recognition That Impermanence Is Normal

Fifth, embracing all the change states that affect us shows how impermanence can be regarded as *homeostasis*—an elegant way of saying that the only thing that stays the same is change. Impermanence is normal, impermanence is natural. And as we've already seen when we whimsically tried to visualize what a permanent world would look like, change, and only change, makes the world possible. Change is the rule; we may not like this rule, we may spend our lives refusing to bow down to it, but that doesn't make it less of a rule.

Living in the "Now"

Sixth, a great benefit of *bardo* knowledge is that it keeps us in the "now." Not just in the 24-hour "today" of a 12-Step program, but right here, *right now*. Perhaps the only way to stay afloat in the eddies and maelstroms of concurrent *bardo* states is to collapse the ones that are painful and embrace the ones that are beneficial and positive. This requires self-knowledge and the ability to learn from yesterday and to look forward to tomorrow—but to do our living in the "now." After all, "now" is all we have.

So, is it possible to truly know and understand The Truth of Impermanence? Perhaps. Sogyal Rinpoche, author of *The Tibetan Book of Living and Dying*, gives us the prescription:

> Ask yourself these two questions: Do I remember at every moment that I am dying, and everyone and everything else is, and so treat all beings at all times with compassion? Has my understanding of death and impermanence become so keen and so urgent that I am devoting every second to the pursuit of enlightenment? If you can answer "yes" to both of these, then you have really understood impermanence.

EPILOGUE

Thus the case is made to place grief into a much larger context. We've solidified what we know about the way grief is treated in the West, and we've taken a leap of faith toward Eastern philosophy. It is clear that we must rearrange how we think (or should think) about anger, depression, grief, and states of change.

As psychotherapists, we cannot continue to treat anger and depression outside the context of a grief stage. While anger and depression may appear to be stand-alone issues, they are, in fact, certified, bona fide stages of grief, and they should always be dealt with as such. Although we have not been trained to see anger and depression as grief stages, although the *Diagnostic & Statistical Manual IV* doesn't recognize this relationship, and although the client may deny or otherwise fail to see that their anger or depression is related to grief, we aren't helping a patient if we fail to help him or her discover all the concurrent grief stages that he or she is in; the unspoken loss that hangs over the client's head like a cloud.

Bereavement is merely the most visible of the many dozens of *bardo* states that, like sound waves, light waves, and subatomic particles, surround us at all times. Were therapists to understand that acute grief is the canary in the mineshaft of *bardo* states, they would see that coping with The Truth of Impermanence is one of the great motivators of mankind. We run toward food, warmth, and shelter, but we expend even more energy running from impermanence.

By putting all anger and depression under the term *grief*, then sliding grief under *acute and chronic bardo states*, we're saying life's impermanence leads to dozens of major and minor life changes, and acute grief is where it bubbles to the top. It's the pool of oil that alerts us to riches beneath the surface. Our patients present in our treatment centers and psychotherapy offices complaining of anger and depression. We treat these symptoms with medication and talk therapy, but we merely skim the surface of the central problem. We have given them palliative care under the guise of true treatment.

Why are therapists doing this? Because most fear impermanence themselves and don't like dealing with the fragility of life. Like their patients, they are in the dark about big and small *bardo* states, and together they blindly engage in a therapeutic relationship that merely appears to have solved a problem. A *bardo* state of anxiety collapses and opens up another that continues to cause pain.

Therapists must learn to do their best to embrace The Truth of Impermanence. They must begin to develop and cultivate a deep, abiding understanding of how truly impermanent life is. This means more than simply practicing a religion that offers us a "Get Out of Time and Into Eternity" card. As humans, we live in time, we raise our families in time, and it's time for psychotherapy to place *time* back in its rightful place. No longer can we hide from it ourselves or allow our clients to shun it. We owe them at least that much.

BIBLIOGRAPHY

Alcoholics Anonymous 4th edition (The AA Big Book). New York: Alcoholics Anonymous World Services, Inc., 2001.

American Psychiatric Association. *Diagnostic & Statistical Manual of Mental Disorders IV* (DSM-IV). Washington, D.C.: American Psychiatric Association, 2000.

Atchley, Robert. "A Continuity Theory of Normal Aging." *Gerontologist* 29, 2 (1989), 183–90.

Bianchi, Eugene. *Aging As a Spiritual Journey*. New York: Crossroad Publications, 1991.

Branden, Nathaniel. *The Six Pillars of Self-Esteem*. New York: Bantam Books, 1994.

Carrubba, Sandy McPherson. "Oklahoma City Bombing: Two Fathers and Forgiveness." *St. Anthony Messenger*, April 2000.

Corey, Gerald. *Theory and Practice of Counseling and Psychotherapy*. Belmont, California: Wadsworth Publishing, 1986.

Evans-Wentz, W. Y. (trans.). *The Tibetan Book of the Dead*. London: Oxford University Press, 1927.

Frankl, Viktor E. *Man's Search for Meaning*. New York: Washington Square Press, 1946.

Freud, Sigmund. "Mourning and Melancholia." In *Metapsychology* 1. London: Pelican Freud Library, 1917.

Gorle, Howard R. *An Introduction to Death and Dying*. 2002 (http://www.bereavement.org, accessed 12 July 2004).

Kübler-Ross, Elisabeth. *On Death and Dying*. New York: Scribner Books, 1969.

Lindemann, Erich. "The Symptomology and Management of Acute Grief." *American Journal of Psychiatry* 101 (September 1944), 141–48.

Lucas, Kenneth. *Outwitting Your Alcoholic.* Ravensdale, Washington: Idyll Arbor, Inc., 1998.

May, Rollo. *Freedom and Destiny.* New York: W. W. Norton & Co., 1981.

Newhouse, Eric. *Alcohol: Cradle to Grave.* Center City, Minnesota: Hazelden Books, 2001.

Nhat Hanh, Thich. *The Heart of the Buddha's Teaching.* Berkeley, California: Broadway Books, 1998.

Rando, Therese. *Grief, Dying and Death.* Champaign, Illinois: Research Press, 1984.

Rinpoche, Sogyal. *The Tibetan Book of Living and Dying.* San Francisco: Harper Collins, 1993.

Ross, Oliver. *Situational Mediation.* Ravensdale, Washington: Idyll Arbor, Inc., 2003.

Snowdon, David. *Aging with Grace, What the Nun Study Teaches Us about Leading Longer, Healthier, and More Meaningful Lives.* New York: Bantam Books, 2002.

Thurman, Robert A. F. (trans.). *The Tibetan Book of the Dead.* New York: Bantam Books (Wisdom Edition), 1994.

White, William L. *Slaying The Dragon.* Bloomington, Illinois: Chestnut Health Systems/Lighthouse Institute, 1998.

Worden, William. *Grief Counseling and Grief Therapy.* New York: Spring Publishing, 1982.

Yalom, Irvin D. *Existential Psychotherapy.* New York: Basic Books, 1980.

Zukav, Gary. *The Dancing Wu Li Masters.* New York: William Morrow & Co., 1979.

0-595-32149-6

Printed in the United Kingdom by
Lightning Source UK Ltd., Milton Keynes
137396UK00001B/319/A